On the work in general

The work of William Pitt Root. . . . has been nourishing my life for years.

—James Wright—

What does a person do to read (work) like Root's? What does he need to possess in order to "understand"? Knowledge of successions of love, puzzles of loyalty, memory . . . . The balance between the poet's offering and the reader's is very shrewd.

—Benjamin DeMott, *New York Times Book Review*

The Unbroken Diamond Nightletter To The Mujahideen, Pipedream Press, Chapbook 1983. (Pushcart Prize, 1984.)

I found this poem to be an extremely strong piece of work deserving to see the light of day—more accurately, the dark of print—immediately: This country needs this badly. As far as I know you are the only man in the whole US who had heart enough to address the subject (of the Soviet invasion of Afghanistan). Your lines may not help much those poor people; but they surely redeem this nation.

—Joseph Brodsky—

This is a 'political' or 'engaged' poem written neither from left nor right, but simply from that human indignation sparked by all oppression. . . . In our age of terror, it forges polemical metal in lyric fire.

—Denise Levertov—

Faultdancing, University of Pittsburgh Press, 1986.

There is a sort of natural truth in William Pitt Root's poems sorely lacking today not only in our poetry but in our consciousness, and lives, the truth of someone seeking purities, trying to be open-eyed before the evidence, and trying to find what redeems that evidence. What redeems it in Root's poems are sympathy, genuine emotion, intensity of vision, and a rigorous exclusion of the merely sentimental and easily received. These works are of the real world, outer and inner, but they intensify that world, and ground it in its movements toward us.

—C. K. Williams—

Reasons for Going It on Foot, Atheneum, 1981

William Pitt Root's poetry is about the gentle and tenacious nourishment of life. His poems are as quiet and knowledgeable as boulders, but are rung with compassion and longing, and so are human. They break winter's back.

—Barry Holstun Lopez—

What impresses is the depth and diversity of Root's subtle appreciation of the poet's dual roles as spiritual legislator and beholder of the physical world.

—*Chicago Sun-Times*—

Reasons is a fully-mature, deeply-felt document [whose] range is exceedingly wide. Throughout, I am impressed by the antipodes of Root's masculinity and the delicate nature of his art. The contrast is embodied in "For The World's Strongest Man," about an Olympic Champion weight-lifter who also gardens and has developed hybrids of roses and tomatoes. Root states about the weight-lifter, and presumably about himself, "What a man would grow must flourish first in his heart." And what a big heart it is!.

—Robert Phillips, *Hudson Review*—

Invisible Guests, Confluence Press, 1984.

Few poets are as aware as Root of their origins. Here Root shares his uncanny sympathy for others... (and) touches them often with his deepest feelings. He is that rare poet who can write of the macho life...(yet) is unafraid to express his feelings. What a gift these magical poems are! Root's humanity is inspired, gentle, and profound.

—Robert Peters—

John Gardner wrote that fiction can be moral only if the writer cares about his or her characters. Let me introduce you to a new one: Coot. Part curmudgeon and part fool, Coot seems to be drawn from the lore and legend that is part of the collective unconscious of our own American West—the mountain man, the old prospector, grizzled and part crazy.

—National Public Radio—

Root is a craftsman not only in the construction of individual poems but in the orchestration of his books. This is the magic of a poet who has earned our faith.

—H. A. Maxon, *Quarterly West*—

In the World's Common Grasses, Moving Parts, Santa Cruz, 1981

This is one of the rare books of contemporary poetry in which there is a trinity of real love: for his father, his daughter, and the supreme eloquence with which he writes about each. . . . William Pitt Root is probably one of the most honest poets of his generation.

—*Small Press Review*—

Whitman's *Leaves of Grass* comes to mind. . . . If ever a poetry collection were to speak to the common man's experience, this is it.

—*The Midwest Book Review*—

Striking the Dark for Music, Atheneum, 1973

What Root is charting is a process of growth, the growth of an individual consciousness that necessarily begins in self-centeredness but makes it way steadily toward a more cosmic awareness. The wholeness of *Striking* is a reflection of the wholeness of Root's vision, which ranges from the deeply personal to the mythic.

—T. R. Hummer—

"Songs" Root calls them, by which he means nothing so recuperable as verse, nothing so predictable as prosody. . . . So solicited, you like such a voice, or you don't. I do like it.

—Richard Howard, *North American Review*—

The Storm and Other Poems, Atheneum, 1969

Recent anthologies of the work of young poets resemble in many ways a one-ring circus with poet as small-time acrobat, clown, and popcorn peddler. It is our gain that William Pitt Root has refused to join the circus and has chosen rather to demand of his art an honesty and boldness that mark his poems as the work of a serious writer . . . . One has the strong feeling that here is a poet who has been near something important, near enough to have been so haunted that poetry was the inevitable result.

—*Virginia Quarterly*—

TRACE ELEMENTS
from a Recurring Kingdom

Other Works by William Pitt Root

POETRY

Trade Editions

Faultdancing, 1986
Invisible Guests, 1984
Reasons for Going It on Foot, 1981
Striking the Dark Air for Music, 1973
The Storm and Other Poems, 1969

Limited Editions

Seagrape Tree & The Miraculous, 1986
The Unbroken Diamond: Nightletter
  to the Mujahideen, 1983
In The World's Common Grasses, 1981
Fireclock, 1981
Coot and Other Characters, 1977
A Journey South, 1977
7 Mendocino Songs, 1977

Translation

Kingdom of Quick Song: Selected Odes of Pablo Neruda, 1994

Edited Anthologies

Timesoup: Poems, Stories, and Graphics by
  Young Alaskans; with Diane Katsiaficas, 1979
Whataworld, Whataworld: Poems by Young People, 1975

COLLABORATION

The Port of Galveston, 1976

FILMS

7 For A Magician, with Ray Rice, 1976
Song of the Woman and the Butterflyman,
  with Ray Rice, 1975

TRACE ELEMENTS
from a Recurring Kingdom:
The First Five Books

The Storm and Other Poems

Striking the Dark Air for Music

Reasons for Going It on Foot

Invisible Guests

In the World's Common Grasses

WILLIAM PITT ROOT

A James R. Hepworth Book

CONFLUENCE PRESS / LEWISTON, IDAHO

ACKNOWLEDGEMENTS

These poems have appeared, sometimes in slightly different form, in the following collections, limited editions, chapbooks: THE STORM AND OTHER POEMS (Atheneum, 1969), STRIKING THE DARK AIR FOR MUSIC (Atheneum, 1973), 7 FOR A MAGICIAN (Freestone, 1975), COOT AND OTHER CHARACTERS (Confluence, 1977), 7 MENDOCINO SONGS (Mississippi Mud, 1977), SHEAF POEMS: COLLECTED BROADSIDES (Pipedream Press, 1977), REASONS FOR GOING IT ON FOOT (Atheneum, 1981), IN THE WORLD'S COMMON GRASSES (Moving Parts, 1981), 4 POEMS (Mesilla Press, 1983), INVISIBLE GUESTS (Confluence, 1984).

Originally this work appeared in the following periodicals: ARION'S DOLPHIN, THE ATLANTIC MONTHLY, BELOIT POETRY JOURNAL, BERKSHIRE REVIEW, BLUE LIGHT, BLUE MOON NEWS, BLUE UNICORN, BROWN BAG (Greensboro), CATALYST (Greensboro), CHICAGO REVIEW, CHOWDER REVIEW, CIMMARON REVIEW, COLUMBIA, CORADDI, CUTBANK, COUNTER/MEASURES, FIRST ISSUE (Brattleboro), FLORIDA QUARTERLY, FLY BY NIGHT, FREE FAMILY NOTES, GREENSBORO REVIEW, GREENFIELD REVIEW, HARPERS, HUDSON REVIEW, JEOPARDY, MALAHAT REVIEW (Canada), MASSACHUSETTS REVIEW, MENDOCINO DAILY PLANET, MID-AMERICAN REVIEW, MISSISSIPPI MUD, THE NATION, NEW YORKER, NORTH AMERICAN REVIEW, NORTHWEST REVIEW, ONE WORLD (Scotland), OREGONIAN, POETRY NOW, PIPEDREAM PRESS PENNYPAPER, PLACE, POETRY (Chicago), POETRY KANTO (Japan), QUARTERLY WEST, THE RHODE ISLANDER, SEATTLE REVIEW, SEIZURE, SEWANEE REVIEW, SHENANDOAH, SLACKWATER REVIEW, SOUTHEAST ARTS JOURNAL (England), SOUTHWEST REVIEW, SOUTHERN POETRY REVIEW, SPOOR, STAR ROOT, STONECLOUD, THREE RIVERS POETRY JOURNAL, UZZANO, VANDERBILT REVIEW, VIRGINIA QUARTERLY, WRITERS FORUM, YAKIMA, YARROW; and/or in the following anthologies: ACADEMY OF AMERICAN POETS ANTHOLOGY 1969, AMERICAN CLASSIC: CAR POEMS, AN AMERICA'S ANTHOLOGY: A GEOPOETICS LANDMARK, ANTHOLOGY OF MAGAZINE VERSE AND YEARBOOK OF AMERICAN POETRY 1981 & 1985, BLUE DUN, BORESTONE MOUNTAIN BEST POEMS OF 1974, BRIDGES: POETS OF THE HUDSON VALLEY, CROSSING THE RIVER: POETS OF THE AMERICAN WEST, A DECADE OF POEMS FROM SOUTHERN POETRY REVIEW, EAST COAST POETS, 80 FOR THE 80'S, FACES OF POETRY, FLOATING GALLERY, THE GENERATION OF 2000: 30 CONTEMPORARY POETS, THE GREAT PLAINS ANTHOLOGY, GREENSBORO READER, INTRO 2, THE LAST BEST PLACE: A MONTANA ANTHOLOGY, LOTUS IN THE STONE, MICHIGAN SIGNATURES, THE MORROW BOOK OF YOUNG AMERICAN POETS, NEW VOICES IN AMERICAN POETRY, NEW YORKER BOOK OF POEMS, ONLY IN HER SHOES: POEMS ABOUT WOMEN AGING, ORACLE: A VOLUNTARY, POETRY BRIEF, PUSHCART PRIZE ANTHOLOGY 1977, 1982, 1984; RAIN IN THE FOREST, LIGHT IN THE TREES: A GATHERING OF CONTEMPORARY NORTHWEST POETS; RED CLAY READERS 3 & 5, "SINCE FEELING IS FIRST," SOUTHWEST: A CONTEMPORARY ANTHOLOGY, SPELLCRAFT, THE SPIDER ANTHOLOGY, STRONG MEASURES: CONTEMPORARY POETS IN TRADITIONAL FORMS, THE UNCOMMON TOUCH, VITAL SIGNS, WHERE WE ARE: THE MONTANA POETS ANTHOLOGY. I also wish to acknowledge Rosa Guy's excellent CHILDREN OF LONGING as the source for "Why That Black Girl Picking Delta Cotton Will Be A Nurse."

And I here reaffirm my gratitude to the following, all of which provided for me as I wrote this work: Galveston Arts Center, Guggenheim Foundation, Mayday Farm (Vermont), National Endowment of the Arts, Rancho Linda Vista (Arizona), Rockefeller Foundation, Stanford University, Tai Farm (California). In addition, I still owe thanks to certain individuals who, one way or another, helped get this work off my desk and into the world: Wendell Berry, Keith Browning, Fred Chappell, Harry Ford, Don Hall, Jim Hepworth, Felicia Rice, Ray Rice, Allen Tate, Peter Taylor, Joel Weinstein.

Publication of this book is made possible, in part, by grants from the Idaho Commission on the Arts, a State agency, and the National Endowment for the Arts in Washington D.C., a federal agency, and the support of Lewis-Clark State College.

FIRST EDITION

99 98 97 96 95   5 4 3 2 1

Library of Congress Card Number: 94-71360
ISBN 1-881090-11-6 (paper) / 1-881090-12-4 (cloth)

Published by:
Confluence Press
Lewis-Clark State College
Lewiston, Idaho 83501

Distributed to the trade by:
National Book Network
4720-A Boston Way
Lanham, Maryland 20706

Dedication

I dedicate this book to the living
through whom I pass
    and to the living and dead
    from whom I've sprung

    I dedicate this book to loving
    and beloved friends,
        old and new
        and yet to come,

        and I dedicate this book to anyone
        who, having read it,
            enjoys returning
            to such company.

        But this book is especially
        for Pamela
            whose loving company
            I so enjoy.

CONTENTS

XI. ON THE OTHER SIDE OF THE EARTH

Preface:

*Notes On Arrangement, Revisions, The Glass House,
Charging Rhinoes and Such*

Rearrangements

When a friend from Sweden recently visited, we consulted a
world map so he could show me his new hometown. He was
startled to see that on my map the Americas occupy its center,
with Europe as right wing, Asia as left. "You put America at the
center of your maps?" he asked, amazed.

"And what do you put at the center of yours?"

"Well"—and by now we were both trying not to laugh—
"Sweden, of course!"

When assembling a book at any given point in one's life,
whatever seems central becomes the center, with individual
poems laid out around that pivot. But time passes, other pivots
suggest themselves. And though these pivots ultimately are all
jars on hills in Tennessee, or hubs in the wheel whose center is
everywhere, they serve. So, in *Trace Elements from a Recurring King-
dom* I've broken up some previous patterns while keeping others.

The long title sequence of *Striking the Dark Air For Music* is for
the most part untouched, as is the bulk of *Invisible Guests*, though
the "Coot" sequence now stands on its own. Coot's not much for
assimilation.

I've redistributed the work from *The Storm and Other Poems* and
Reasons For Going it On Foot, the earliest and latest collections.
Poems from each comprise most of *In The World's Common Grasses*,
where mirroring concerns and the mesh of the poems feel more
telling. My own father's death when I was eleven had left me

little to know him by, a fading zone inhabited now by poetic reconstructions, so as my daughter approached that age I experienced an overwhelming desire to provide evidence of my feelings for her more substantial and less perishable than young memories.

Other works from *Reasons, The Storm,* and the preamble poems of *Striking The Dark Air For Music,* are now set into elemental groups: I was raised by the Everglades "Near The Gulf"; from adolescence on, I have lived in the "West," my chosen home, whenever possible (sometimes even when it's only barely possible—just now I teach in Manhattan but commute from Tucson). "Love," "Creatures," and "Art" sustain me when all else blurs, hence those sections. The poems opening and closing this collection are what they seem: ways into and out of the recurring kingdom.

Why "kingdom" in an age when social orders everywhere are yawing and collapsing back into commonalities and aristocracies are regularly under seige? Because in its earliest formative stages a psyche may be innocent of history but not of magic, and I was raised in what I took for a kingdom, a place and way soon shattered but elementally charged and resurgent.

Revisions

Not only have I rearranged the order of many of these poems—I've also taken the opportunity to revise a number of them. In some cases, such as "Dear Jeffers" and "The Names Of The Dead," I've changed lineation, cut lines. In others I've repaired punctuation, desparate rhymes, weak images that have bothered me for years. I have also added three new poems: the opener (a natural), "Making Way," and one poem new to the "Coot" sequence. I also played around with dropping this one or that one but finally restored them all, trusting posterity to be the better editor.

Writer and Reader

It is considered unseemly, unwise, for poets to comment upon their poems, in part because once published they are no longer the poet's and come to have lives and meanings of their own, just as children do, evolving through mysteries of which their progenitors may know very little.

That said, nonetheless I venture this observation about the Reckoning poems of the *Striking* sequence. While they were written prior to a divorce, no small part of my quarrel was—as many, perhaps, of our quarrels are—with myself. Myselves. The "you" and "I," the X and Y of those poems may be read as the dark and light halves of one entity reestablishing its boundaries through dialogue, even through agony. The immediate results of those shifts in a balance of power may be read in the Songs which follow. Others, Roethke and Berryman among them, have worked this psychic arena; more recently, Joy Harjo refigured this *terra infirma* with her ritualistic "She Had Some Horses," an enchanted poem which concludes,

> She had some horses she loved.
> She had some horses she hated.
>
> These were the same horses.

I hazard these remarks partly because readers bearing in mind the possibilities of such a mirroring may find that sequence more interesting than those who read it solely as domestic debris.

It is always a delight to have a reader remark about a poem in such a way as to indicate that synchronous parallels do exist in connections no conscious intention could ever achieve. Visiting a workshop of Bill Stafford's in Tulsa in 1980, I was astonished when one student introduced himself to me by saying from heart an uncollected poem of mine published a decade earlier in *100 Flowers*, a journal that lasted one issue. For such luck, one may be grateful if not proud.

One does not come to a poem searching for the poet so much as in search of lost or emergent aspects of one's self. This may even be a part of what underlies the spontaneous litmus test by which we intuitively distinguish between what is personal and what is merely private in poems.

"How Do You Write?": Rhinoes and Commas

How do you write? is one of those perennial questions that suggests a perennial interest, so I'll say something about that. I'm never sure if the questioner expects an answer of the Flaubertian "Oh it's very grueling—I'll spend all morning putting a comma in and all afternoon taking it out" variety, or hopes to hear "Between shots at the charging rhino I dashed off a tanka in blood on my thigh." The truth, as always, is neither, but a bit of each.

The earliest work here, from 1963, "In Late Winter," "End of a Season," "Holocaust," is apprentice work in forms and came out of delightfully grueling sessions of many concentrated hours each, with endless tinkering until each was, like a pie, done. The validation that comes from satisfactorily completing a quatrain or an entire sonnet can be exquisite for anyone exploring the craft. That level of concern changed abruptly with the birth of our daughter in 1965 which triggered many poems— "On the Tidal Ledge," "Jellyfish," "The Visiting Hour"—that took me beyond a sense of the primacy of craft so that revisions, still arduous, revolved around loosening forms to let substance breath more freely. During my year and a half at M.F.A. studies I finished my first book and began the second, writing furiously and constantly.

"The Storm" (1966) required six months. I started it in response to memories evoked by the scents of an on-coming summer rainstorm in North Carolina. Each of the first several sections was a "false start" I abandoned to try again with the next section. When it occurred to me to use all of the bits and pieces, I was excited but soon stymied about what should follow, and the poem stalled until I dreamed the dream in part six, which then carried me through. "Circle of Struggle," in contrast, took two or three days. It began as an exercise to move away from the thinly veiled blank verse line of "The Storm" by emulating William Carlos Williams' more dynamic free verse line, but the poem soon ran off on its own.

Most of the work in the *Striking* sequence came very quickly, often a poem or two, even three a day. After the publication of *The Storm and Other Poems* in 1969, I determined not to repeat the elegiac strain of that work, but to write in first person, present tense. The first line that came was "I am empty."

Years before, while I was still in my sonnet-villanelle stage, John Logan had urged me to submit work to Robert Bly. I did, and he responded "Empty." Jean Renoir, the film-maker, once said, "Fear is my compass," and I tried to follow his lead. I took that dark judgement to be my polestar, daring the demons, and soon enough found there was no bottom to such a descent. I had, as Rilke put it, "to change my life." With that resolve, the Songs began to flow, alternating with the Reckonings at first, then replacing them altogether. All the while the poems came hard and fast. Longer lines replaced shorter, rhythms began to open like the lassoe of Pecos Bill when he presumed to rope the moon. And like that Bill, I began to feel I'd overextended myself. Then, for a year, nearly two, nothing.

When those poems were about to be published in 1973, I was living cheap in an off-season vacation home just south of Mendocino, "The Glass House." It perched yards from a cliff and its all-glass front made me feel like I'd live forever each morning when I woke and saw once again the sea rolling toward me, the rising fog, the otters at work in the bay opening abalones on their skyward bellies, the hawks and gulls, the migrating whales. And my daughter was living nearby so I saw her often. It was heaven. And I started to write again: short lyrics, narratives. . . . All the stuff the preceding years had stored mute in me began to flow and flood. I wrote much of *Invisible Guests* and the entire collection *Faultdancing* in two or three months (for various reasons the latter wouldn't be published until 1986). But jobs were almost impossible to find locally. One day I stood on the nearby bridge with a dime to my name, looking out at the expanse of sea and coast that has never failed to wing my heart, and I tossed that dime into the river, saying to whatever angels out there might take my call, "I've never been so happy in my life and I need help bad." The next day I got a letter from the National Endowment for the Arts congratulating me on having received a grant.

Most of my rhinoes have been financial. Once when an interviewer asked that old question, "Why do you write poems?" I was only mildly surprised to hear my answer: "So I'll never have to deal with the temptations of being rich." Happily, temptations abound nonetheless.

W.P.R.

I. WORKING BY THE RIVER OF LOST SOULS

Working by the River of Lost Souls

That's a poetic title, nonetheless true
if you take the local histories for true,
but the Animas at flood is definitely muddy
with earth washed down from upriver slopes
as I'm working out a new table of contents
for the book you're holding now, when my dog,
Oscar, growls.
        "Hey, mister, what shoe dune?"
asks a skinny fellow unsteady on bowlegs.
"Is that insurance papers or something?"
We talk and I can see he's thirsty for
more of the thing that's got him wobbling
and my heart sinks. He's been on the road
a long time, lost his pack and cash at
a bus stop in Boise. He's been to Detroit,
St. Louis, Tulsa—"I seen it all, like the eagle
of my people" he says, then asks if I believe
in Christ. "I take that dude for my saviour."
The river rushing in front of us is just
the color of his face. I point out a mallard
bobbing through rapids just as it takes off
then he points to three more riding easier
currents next to shore. "Some take it easy,
some go for the gusto. I like to live every
minute every day," he proclaims. "Like the
bald eagle of my people." "Well, I'm about
bald as an eagle," I offer, smiling, but not him,
he's watching the river. "You're no eagle, bro."
I don't argue. He grins. "So let's hear a poem."
And I read one about watching a baby pigeon
sitting oblivious in a bullsnake's mouth
as the snake slowly swallows and how we
can do nothing for such a one but witness
its fate. He likes it, we shake hands in
a clumsy three-part handshake that ends
clasping wrists. He asks for money for coffee
and I give him a dollar. Before he leaves
he tosses back his head and his eyes
above the broad cheekbones gleam. "Maybe
one day you'll write about me?"

II.   NEAR THE GULF

"light that had once seemed sufficient"

Wheel Turning on the Hub of the Sun

I was young.
      A hundred yards off at the edge of the reflective mud
tall white birds like spirits gathered for a ceremony
stalked slowly along the bottom
as the surface of the pond gave back the dance.
Each strode in the pool of its own image
and the queer noises they made
made the silence deeper.

The sun was a member of their dance and the trees
lent shadows to the edges of the pond shimmering
like water in a saucer tipped.

What I can remember now
comes as from a dream glowing in the mind until it's
spoken of, and goes away. I know
that they strode in their dance for hours
and drew their long yellow legs up into the commotion of
      their wings
and rose in a great circle overhead, their wheel
above me turning on the hub of the sun
—and that when they were gone, standing like one
in a darkness after lightning
in the light that once had seemed sufficient,
I found myself alone.

                      —Everglades, Florida—

Field Late in Fall

The dry sleeves of the corn stalks
flap and rattle, alive with gestures
of wind, as the wired black feet
of the glistening crows hold fast.

Bobbing and swaying on hollow spines,
they bow when the stalks are bowed by wind
that whines in their black empty beaks.
Their eyes glitter with ants and beetles.
Above them, the living call and wheel.

The Wavering Field

The plow has stunned the farmer's hands with callous.
Waiting for the boy, he attempts to balance
his body's exhaustion with the land's. From above
the sun's oceanic glare discovers
the wavering field, where seeds root in the waste
of crops plowed under. He runs with sweat,
his face and raised arm gleam. Both feet
hidden in the broken earth, he leans
against the stock and shades his eyes—his legs
a clay of sweat and dust smoked from the acres
his plow has cut—to watch his youngest son,
real against the shimmering horizon,
run from the house and past the family graveyard.
A mason jar of water shines in his arms.

Whiskey Creek Bridge

Standing on the wooden bridge at Whiskey Creek
where my father's old and new farms meet and join,
I listen for a moment: everything is silent
save mosquitoes and the stiff dry-sounding dragonflies
that skim the water's smooth back for dark specks.

Below me, poised and waiting
in silver webs that flex under the bridge,
huge spiders shine and dangle in the dark,
the harmlessly exotic and the deadly,
a black widow looming by the dry shell of her mate,
her womb filled with seed fed by its father's flesh,
the hourglass of blood set in her belly.

Where water clear as amber runs,
I watch the sluggish traffic from the swamps
drain toward the Gulf: cypress branches wrapped in moss,
    half sunk,
rigid garfish, mullet in dull swarms, cottonmouths and perch,
broad leaves turning slowly in the underwater light
and a variety of turtles—some soft-shelled and graceful,
some with brilliant faces, orange and yellow streaked
as if their budshaped heads were splitting into bloom,
and some, harder, darker, whose horned beaks crack
the others' shells and ream them while they die—,
all moving downstream to feed the broad Caloosahatchee
where fresh water and salt collide and mingle,
where seabirds, sand sharks and bull gators wait.

When a branch snaps and falls, breaking the surface,
I start with the fish, shivers of rising silver
that feign and turn, vanish into the spreading calm
where the shadow of my childhood holds them all,
a darkness deep almost beyond my seeing.

Summer of Morning Glories

Coming back from a childhood creek
on an unlit whirring bike at night
and dizzy with the effort on a hill,
I watch the carlights fan out over trees
dying slowly of massive flowering vines
and turn off on the roadside grass,
glad to rest.

      The cars, like insects,
take the crest and speed past in the dark,
leaving me—a child again, in awe of power
and the driver's solitude—to speculate about
the sharp sound of the crickets' dark machine
or fireflies, like floating stars, rising
from the woods, the road,
and even from the weeds that hold our home.

III. IN THE WORLD'S COMMON GRASSES:

POEMS OF A SON, POEMS OF A FATHER

These poems I dedicate with love to my daughter, Jennifer Lorca, and to the memory of my father, whose name is my own.

Waking to the Comet

You were beside me.
You were the mountain
blocking half
a sky full of stars.

I was small
in the depth of your shadow,
watching black water
and glittering boats.

Everyone sat
on blankets in grass,
drinking and eating,
talking and waiting.

I played, then slept,
until your hand stirred me.
I woke among strangers
all staring up.

High overhead,
faint, among whispers,
floated a figure
with long glowing hair.

You called it by name.
Everyone watched it.
I watched you and mother,
the way your cheeks shone.

Once in a lifetime, *you said,*
soft as breathing,
speaking to no one.
I loved you both then.

I saw mother, crying,
the way her hand glowed

through darkness toward
the ghost of your hand.

Now I am grown.
You've gone to earth.
I have my own child,
and the comet we saw

is just starting back
from a distance much deeper
than I could have guessed
as a boy in the gathering dew.

Closing the Casket

Deep in the calm of a drawing room of flowers,
the only hand my father held
was dead.

       Eleven
I held my mother's hand
wondering how much different mine must feel.
Invisible behind a wreathe of leaves
the Bible shut.

       Her grip tightened
and trembled as her rings cut our flesh
and blood came to the edges
of the stones.

Passage of the Living

Vespers

As a train in the night gains speed,
I wake to darkness, think of light
careering through frail galaxies
of frosted wire and weeds that
glitter and vanish in fields
beyond the town, and farther still
through foothills and the dark passes
blasted from their darker stone
that dangerously lean
against the passage of the living
through the darkness, through the sleep
of children dreaming, men and women dreaming
as the dark cries to their dreams
and their dreams cry back.

Matins

Now the starlit dew burns on the branch
and spins the tree, spins the rooted earth
in planet light, and falls. Brightness burns
the angled stones, consumes the darkness ripe
within the yawing trunks and radiant underleaves.
Dawn burns and the creatures wake
from desperate sleep, and stare.

The Storm

for my mother

1.
My father was a skeptic
but a farmer. He believed
in impossibility—
                    waiting
for the Gulf coast's holocaustal hurricanes,
he'd cut the earth
and seed each fresh wound
with a row of curses,
ram the tractor into gear
and tear his land apart
to put it back together,
                    me beside him
watching, my memory planted
with each season's violent crop, ripening
as each acre ripened.

2.
                    This was near
the Everglades, years ago,
while I was a child learning to live
from a man learning to die.
His life: the steady green profusion
of hot leaves devouring air and light,
sucking rain dark under wide steaming fields
with underground acres of tendrilous roots,
a pale brutal ferocity spreading its strength,
unthinking and gradual.

3.
                    Mondays, coughing blood
in handkerchiefs he buried in his fields,
he'd disappear, the high pitched jingle
of a tailgate chain following
toward Colored Town. There he'd bail
fieldhands out of jail, tallying
that cost against their wages.
He'd disappear, leaving me to stare
at walls the early darkness hid.

                                              I'd hear
my mother tossing into sleep, and often woke
at dawn from dreaming of her stifled moans
and turned my pillow over to protect her
from my tears. Then, watching palms
fixed against the dawn window,
I'd wonder what was wrong
and sleep again.

4.
                    There was great preparation
before storms. When 48-hour warnings came,
he'd hire triple crews at doubled wages,
Puerto Ricans, blacks, whites,
men and their wives, truckloads
of workers laughing at first and singing,
then anxious as the thick sky's clouds
bulged downward through the darkness,
truckload after truckload raising
dust from each storm-colored road.

He did what could be done against disaster.
Every crop that could be picked was picked
—tomatoes, eggplants, corn and gladiolus,
watermelons—everything
ripe enough to save.
                          As I grew
old enough to help, he let me.
I bent down through the hours of song
and through the sting of rain,
picked on through the hour of hush
before the wind, excited by the lull
as others whispered, "It's getting time to stop,
it's time to go."
                      Then the wind would start
and then the leaves turn belly-up,
revealing each green bulge left to the storm.
As distant trucks coughed to life,
"It's time to go!" And large clear drops
like fear fell, chilling our shocked skins.

5.
At home our grass was flattened by the wind.
The ancient palms in front arched and creaked,
fronds flinging like the tails of rushing horses.

The boarded house crouched like a cat. Wind
held my door closed till father helped, then,
pressed against the truck's cold length and awkward,
we crept past the garage to the backyard.
Before he hid in the house, we'd take a leak
and watch wind make it spray for twenty feet.

6.
This is the close time of candles, of windows
black with boards, their cracks blackened by the sky,
when windows are opened to keep the house
from exploding, and even his laughter is silence,
trapped in the dim fragile rooms of our home.
In this last longest storm, I am the candle carrier,
checking every door and window in those rooms
the storm won't let us use. By candlelight
I see rain flicker on the bedroom floors,
and I roll up rugs as coconuts like cannonballs
clatter on the street. I bring us blankets,
pillows, sheets, and secret handkerchiefs
for him.
            At night we sleep in the depths
of the house, and I dream of my father, coughing.
His crops are ripe around him, tall and still.
Behind his back the sun widens and blinds me
as he coughs and crouches, coughing again.
Trying to scream, I am dumb.
                            I see his gladiolus
dying, the wreckage of 10,000 blossoms floating,
wide useless blossoms, ripe and flimsy,
drowning in the armpit deep floodwater
of flowershining lakes. The storm
has flushed out cottonmouths
and alligators, leaving raccoons
to starve on stumps and cypress knees
or to feed from the bobbing carcasses
of rattlesnakes and rabbits, their long black hands
meticulously waking the smooth surface
of a sky pierced, row on row, by phalanxes
of swordlike stalks, the broken harvest
of my father's curses.
                        And as these waters sink,
I come with him although he cannot see me
to slit the throats of pigs, bloated and blacksnouted,
their lips soaked back from white gums

and stained tusks. When the corpses
will not bleed, I stand and watch his anger rip
while my blade, thick with gore,
hangs still and helpless. The stench
of vegetables and flesh is rotten all around us.

He crouches against the sun. Above me
his black shoulders heave. One hand is full of light.
The other hand extends toward me from darkness, gently,
turns away my face and lifts my chin.
I cannot scream, my tongue is dead with fear.
I cannot see his face.
                         Lightning
blinds the room: the storm is over
and I wake.

7.
                    Father, your farm is in the hands
of strangers now, and I, a stranger,
waken in strange rooms filled with your presence
as a sky after lightning is still filled
with the scent of light. Faced with glass,
dismembered by its seams, I see you
gaze at herons on a mudflat at sunset.
For years your shape's been paralyzed
among palmetto silhouettes,
but now you cough—tossing water
like a shower of fire,
a single heron stretches into flight
and through the burning veil of flashing wings
I see you kneel at last.

The living dark curls up around your back
and you are gone, the dark rising around you
as you bend to plant your blood.

But father, O father,
what silence.

End of a Season

As hot light drinks the puddles
from concrete, and gladiolus
rise like knuckled sticks, God's
day, Sunday, burns. The clouds have opened

just enough, and sunlight stares
the shadows into trees. From bushes,
small birds flip through the air,
or peck at thorns bright with bugs,

feeding where branches are open coffins.
On the lawn a mat of cut
grass rots. A shabby robin
yanks a worm that stretches as he tugs.

It snaps. The gladiolus rattle
if you're close enough to hear
and there's a breeze. Ants and beetles
crawl along the leaves like paper.

Of three stalks, two are ragged
with dead flowers. The third is tight
with buds, but dry and almost dead
despite the rain, the gardener, and the light.

Passing a Sawmill at Night

The road was straight. A gully braced by stumps
plunged from the edge. Beyond it a fall field
widened through the darkness toward a clump
of trees in silhouette against the sawmill wall.
Slowing down, I watched the bright smoke
scatter ashes dying among stars.

Years before, with a word spoken,
my father stopped the jeep as we hunted his farm.
Our years together ending, the stubble behind us bright
with frost, we watched a distant mill's dark walls
pulse with swollen squares of fire. "At night,"
he told me (he still moves through the smells
of oil and gunpowder, night itself,
reaching to release the brake), "a man knows
more than he can learn of death, and life."

I stopped the car, slowly. My wife leaned
against my arm, asleep. Across the road,
through the living trees, the taken burned.

The Gulf

How they burn,
the manes of his horses
in the light-torn
waves, like curses

in an ancient dream,
a Viking sailor's
nightmare, brim
with serpents, failures.

From the cliff
the father shouts.
He shouts again,

and hears a laugh
as the surf shifts,
surrounding his son.

Circle of Struggle
for Judith

This morning, when I had to kill
a mouse to free it
from a trap,
I remembered the rat's gnawed foreleg
my father made me see—sheer bone
protruding from a thin
clenched paw. And this was our secret,
father's and mine, kept
from mother, safe in her kitchen,
for years.
           When he died at the verge
of my manhood, she fled north
with me. There I learned the seasons
in a long strange year.
I saw the crippled trees
crumple into colors, shedding
their brilliant disease of leaves
that left the branches dead
and trembling in the snow-white wind,
magical and stark
between streetlamps and starlight.

I learned to set out traps
for muskrats, mink, and rabbits—declaring
I would never marry, never.
And each dawn of the long first winter,
silent in the moonlight, I hiked
through the frostbright
dreamlike sleeping trees
that jutted like black bone
from wounded snow. Alone among
the creatured drifts and banks
piled up in the months between
my father's death and my
own beating flesh,
I was fearful and desirous
of the grey silent wolves
a crushed thing's single shriek
could summon from the dark.

With my strong Confederate bayonet
I'd pry slick frozen steel apart,
freeing stiff legs severed
in my traps. Now and then
a worthless skin.
                        One morning
early in the wind and while
the blowing moon still wobbled,
jostling the dark fixed trunks
of night, I heard a chain snap tight.
Then beating wings. Something white
was fumbling at the base of the trees.

Like snow rising from snow,
a silver fox locked
in its talons, the great white owl rose,
then fell—dragged back by the trapped weight.
Dazzled by the brightening
air, its lunar eyes blazed
in their mask of blind snow
as I tripped on ice, reared
to meet its stare. It challenged:
I froze.
                White breast wide
with the heavy wings of a warrior
angel, it dipped the hook of its beak
in slow deliberation
and stole a vivid eye from the skull,
then turned to me. Impatient,
in an outburst of brilliance,
it battered up
out of the snow, blindly clumsy at first,
then—transfigured by the high light of ascent—
                        aglide
and glowing
                in the pale soaring sky.

Wet blood, bright
in the decomposing snow,
wound in a desperate
circle of struggle, round
and round the strict radius
of the staked chain.

All around me the horizon tensed
for dawn, encircling my vision
with the limits of a saw-toothed land
sharp against the sky,
and from this trap's dead center,
I looked up at the fatal stars
so innocent in their slow prison
of seasons and hours.

This morning, when I
sent my wife and daughter from the room,
they fled as if to witness death
were death itself. *Am I to die?*
—this accusation in their fear
has followed me until
I feel as if my own
is the small nodding skull
I've crushed, and mine
the one bright eye
staring from its ruin.
                    So I
am the child again, facing your candor,
knowing this time you must die,
your face pass into my face,
mine into others. What
shall I tell them, father? What can
we say to these strangers
we have made from our love?

Somewhere,
in the belly of the owl and the earth,
we all stare incessantly from
darkness to darkness soaring.

The House You Looked For

1.
Upstate New York,
         that haunts me still—beginning
our late fall walks in fields of blown gold weeds
and trees blown red and gold.

That time, that trip to your old home,
I saw you young, heard stories of you young as me,
your knickers stuffed with stolen cookies,
booty to share with kids you fought the day before,
the year you spent in bed, the several months
of dying you lived through.

I was proud and frightened.
You frightened me and made me proud
of what I might become, being your son.

One trip north
and our drive in country so much changed
you couldn't find for hours the place
you'd come for us to find.

2.
And now it's merely light wind,
         the long light late in the day,
weeds giving way before you,
         I in your wake in the fields,
seed fastening to my pantlegs, your legs
thrashing free of burrs and the thorns and branches
I was trapped by, you against the sun, you tall
as trees, you graceful with your earned strength moving freely.

Then, in a stand of trees the colors of fire,
the house you looked for: sagging roof, broken door
so jammed you had to force it down
with the whole forest looking on
and I looking on.

Inside, cobwebs everywhere. Antique windows
made the light antique as I heard you dressing upstairs
and your mother downstairs calling you
and down the stairs you came.
The stairs collapsing now at the house's center.

3.
Father, you could dance
and you learned to dance
with pain. They told you
you couldn't walk again.
Young and sure to die,
you lay and wept, wasting
in the bed of a closed room.

Then changed.
          Changed
with such fierce strength
that curse became command.
You lived despite them all.
You rose, you walked, by god
you danced back into life.

I still cry when I hear
how, pale and agonized,
you made them watch you dance.
They did not understand.
You called it dance
and dancing it became.

4.
I will learn that from you.
Your eyes' blue fire burned
with how I came to be.

How true you were, and strong,
and how suddenly gone.

I will redeem your blood.

I promise you your name.

White Horse of the Father, White Horse of the Son

Not the delicate mare who came nosing.
Not the dustdim ironeyed gelding.
This was the one. The bright dancer
who would not approach the fence.

Set in one side of his snowbright face
was the blank blue stare of the sky.
And there in the other, a hazel tunnel.
A swirling of greens and browns that could see.

The hooves were pink as tea-roses,
streaked with the pale of oystershell.
This was the great horse I wanted.
And this was the one for sale!

I wanted to try him alone.
How many moons has the sky?
You insisted my friend ride him too.
And he didn't know how. Didn't know.

My hands crossed the brilliant silk
of his neck as the lips of a prince cross
the princess. Who sleeps in forever.
Who wakes in the world. He woke

to my touch and we raced the proud wind
over grass. Over bushes and ditches.
This was the one, the one my dreams
woke to. Wide-eyed. But my friend,

I could feel him slipping.
Feel him falling back into the grass,
as I reached, too late, for his hand.
As my hand reached backward into the blur

of his wide white face and the grass.
He was gone. By the time I could turn
I had heard your voice in my heart.
No Sir. Not this one. No sale.

Father once a son, son become a father,
you riding now the white stallion of your bones!
It is true that I fell from the horse as your son.
That I rode on. Am still riding.

Holocaust

The burning church shuddered. In the mire of its light
the steeple tumbled. A loosened bell broke
the altar into sparks as stained glass windows
burst. Afterward, sorting through the bright
shards of mosaic stories for Moses' burning
bush, I found an infant Christ whose face
was blank with melted lead. The whole place
stank of scalded ash.
                     A month of spring
conjured the fire of flowers from shrubs scarred
by the blaze. Some stiff, fire-scalded leaves
were dead, black on top and pale underneath,
but half-bushes bloomed. And now charred
twigs kink toward the church's shell
while blossoms nod like innocents near hell.

Song of Shaking
for Bill Ransom

Today out in the woods
  an old tree found me.
It said I am you

and a chorus of whispers
blew by where I shook.

I am you *it said*
with no words, no words.

Big tree, dead, huge memory
of itself collapsing
to feed the green shoots
ringing its base,

and the babble of whispers
blew by where I listened,

their small voices hard
to hear:
      We *they seemed to say*
      we
      are becoming you.

And the shaking stopped.

Firstborn

Our first child
     was early, "easy"
they told her, and telling me
     she smiled,
pretended to smile. The pillow case
was white, the sheet stains hidden, her face

familiar, strange.
     And full of guilt
beyond delivery, I felt
     as strange
as Adam joining Eve, feigning pride
while I brought her a rose bright as blood.

The Visiting Hour

As I drove the road I raced the night before,
my headlight's steady glaring hid the stars.
They weren't yet sure our seven-month daughter
could live. I'd known her first night, her horror

muffled by the glass room and Isolette,
the crescent bruises where forceps took her face.
I smoked as I drove, smelling the room where I'd waited,
its shallow cactus of dead cigarettes,

the insurance salesman whose daughter wouldn't breathe.
I was leaning against a curve when I saw the eyes.
I braked and swerved but felt the thud and cry
before I could stop. I looked and found a piece

of bleeding fur, wedged in the front bumper.
The bright racoon was gone; dead, or perhaps
—stunned and hidden in the roadside grass—
waiting till I left to move, or whimper.

Where headlights turned the trunks of trees to stone,
I made my frightened search through weeds. I knew
the racoon lived, but only shadows moved
as I passed the dark curve later, driving home.

Jennifer by Moonlight

A cricket with a short circuit
whirs in grass behind a stone.

The dark electric sound
seems to shine,

attracting our daughter with her
mouthful of moth-wings

toward the porch's edge
where she teeters

on her hands and knees, inarticulate,
and stares.

When a second cricket sizzles
like a star

dunked in a dipper,
she giggles first,

then jabbers at the moon perched
on our Ford.

Carelessly it spills its light
like milk across the yard.

Absorbed
in what she cannot comprehend,

our speechless lady pouts,
vexed

by this brief innocence
of crickets singing and the moon.

From the First and Lasting Dream

As I hear crickets threaten from the dark
beyond our window and watch the moon's
old hunt among sharp branches, my wife
curls in her own deep warmth and stillness.

The car is ours, the house well on its way
to being ours. Whatever ruins memory
has ruined mine: these woods have no beasts left,
my life no fairytales I can forget.

There is a train that sometimes comes
to shake these woods, a loudly prying iron worm
whose windowed belly glows with fetal heads.
Once I dreamed of trains, and how the distance
changes, but worry now: What if the child wakes,
or cannot wake?
                              Chilled in the silent instant,
I see the small lit moonstunned form.

I wake my wife who gently moves now
out of sleeping innocence
and shapes to me, conforms,
admitting deeply the proud surge
that must come with death's urgency
through every generation of desire.

Slowly, Lord, and surely, from the first
and lasting dream shall issue all
our sudden lives, shaped of flesh,
conceived in loss, and driven by desire.

A Start

I first recognized spring
today: holding
my daughter's flowersmeary hands
in my workwooden hands,

I felt
the green blades cocked
in dry wood
drive free.

A Year Has Passed Already, So
for Tim Riley

Sidestepping the amenities, we leave our wives
awkward with each other in the house,
and balancing our glasses of bright wine,
settle as if forever into a frail pair of lawnchairs
that creak and lean and threaten to collapse.
The yard in back—tall with dandelions tilting
in a shimmer of warm wind—hums with bees
that bumble on dull pollen-fluffy thighs
and blurring wings back and forth
to a hive hung like the moon in woods behind us.

Higher on the hill, the steady sound of traffic,
and below, the bursting of waves white against black rocks
rises muffled through wild vines and roses
blossoming between us and a sheer fall to the sea,
the two sounds, at that distance, hard to distinguish.

Watching from the windows, our wives,
still strangers, crowd words about the children
into the leveling silence of neat rooms
where they are held by manners. Our daughters
trade their toys and blows, shyly, with clumsy hands.

We drink and talk as drunken bees
stumble among the yellow sunlit crowns of wild flowers
sprung up in your absence, all but hidden
by June grass I haven't cut yet in July.

By dusk we are quiet, easy with each other,
still among the drowsy pollenated blossoms
abandoned by the bees at last, moonlit, slowly
closing in the dim light at our feet.

Living It Up
While the Wife Is with Her Folks

I hear my watch ticking in the June grass
as my dog leans its head against a fast
thumping foot, and then rolls over.
Paper-littered waves slop below
our dock, and splattered brace-planks gleam.

The blonde who rents next door seems
to wave as she cleans her picture window,
using a sponge and a rubber glove that's yellow.
I feel I could wave back, so I stare
as she polishes the glass. However, finished there,

she moves from sight to a window on the side.
Behind a corner of the house her body hides
as her busy arm wipes on, detached. And when a
sparrow twitters from her T-V antenna,
the dog whimpers, gnawing at another flea.

A dog's life, I mutter, and turn to see
a runabout riding on a crown of white water.
The crowd aboard is sporting all the colors
of the flag that flaps on the stern above the wake.
The people in it wave. Finally I wave back,

and listen to the ticking June grass.

With My Wife Beside the Washougal River, Still Stranded During the Fifth Week of an Airlines' Strike
for Glenn

All day now I've been restless,
camera in hand, waiting
    while the day burns slowly clear
    and wishing I could say just
what I want of you.

This is frightening, to be so far
from how we live or want
    to live. The weeks take
    my desire to think
away. We came

to see the friends
we only write all year, and spoke
    of how we show our age
    by saying they show theirs,
laughed

but could not sleep. The sky
is clear now and your face is buried
    in sleep.... Our friends are gone.
    Remember one, his photographs
    of stone?

Checking In

at 1 A.M., dead tired,
I watch two strangers
carry out a third
across their shoulders,
stiff as a board.

In the step-down lobby,
two whores and a jealous queer
ignore the body
as its eyes open to stare
at me, and these roses for my lady.

An elevator grinds me up
to 3. Stepping off
I breathe again and stop
to check directions: Snuff
and canned spaghetti smells, pop

bottles along a hall
of dead wallpaper flowers. The slick carpet
creaks along the narrow darkness full
of doors locked on regret,
sneak-thieves, and the wounded who can crawl.

Playing Until Dark

Spiraling down out of the Guggenheim,
our daughter packed on my back and giddy still
from her first encounter with the colors
of Chagall, whirling in the eye
of Wright's great twister, we venture past
Good Humor men and into Central Park.

Here bums and tourists, the wealthy's hired nursemaids
free of Harlem until dark, and men retired
from everything are gathered on benches
with fallen leaves.

We are tired, too, and come here to forget
what time it is and where we are. The child
is our only innocence, and here this afternoon
on the dry grass of a park, we play at being young
while she believes us.
                    Above and behind us
on a boulder half-hidden by trees,
a man on his haunches squats to photograph
a friend who masturbates. His picture
will include us at a distance, playing in the park.
He has made us strangers to ourselves
and strangers to our daughter in the silence
that has stopped our game. We move on,
and trees conceal their figures on the stone.

Beyond the lined-up benches, we take a path
descending to a lake. All around are nurses,
families picnicking, men asleep with newspapers
and women sitting near them, alone, staring
beyond their children and each other
into those waters of their world
where sullen swans bask, adrift
in the breakage of their own reflections.

Starlings

Like cones that screech they fill the barren trees.
They think it's spring. I've seen them huddle, huge
with snow-clogged feathers, on withered vines outside
our bedroom window. I heard them late one night,
and rose to watch the whirling dark alone.
They think it's spring. A thaw exposes garbage
in dirt-pitted banks of snow that waste to molds
and curves of sensuous ice. I hold the marriage
ring my flesh has warmed, its weight, and hear,
midwinter, starlings sing that starve.

Heading Home

I am driving with you through the dark
between your home with your mother
and your home with me. Through
the interval, you try to stay awake
to help me stay awake, talking
all the months since our last journey
into hours as precious and disconnected
as our times together are, until you curl
up with the dog you love who licks
you into sleep cuddling
while she breathes
with you, until I cannot tell
which I hear whimper softly
for the other.
                    Fields drift by,
bridges, curves speeding
through the low *om*
of the tires over moonlit asphalt
widening through forests that twinkle
with the eyes of sons and daughters
everywhere, witnessing our passage.

"William," you mumble
from the backseat. "William?"
And, "Yes,"
I answer. *Yes.*

Keeping the Promise

Loving me, knowing my love
of the colors and smells of fresh flowers,
you used the hours we had here
to sack the garden, plundering
roses and dandelions alike
for the blossoms to please me.

When I returned you to your mother
I came back here and found
the dry vase with its dried bouquet
half on the desktop, half still hanging on.

Now I bring in fresh flowers
and keep the others, too, in their vase of air
—here fresh flowers and here your promise
for fresh flowers kept constantly
to cheer me.

A Natural History of Unicorns and Dragons
My Daughter and I Have Known
Written for her 11th birthday

Already we are both fans of the green and golden dragon
   who tumbles gloriously out of the terrible heavens
      not only in books and dreams

for us—He cascades also down the side of the seagreen '61
   Valiant we painted once together by the ocean,
      trying to outrace the setting Mendocino sun

four years ago with mist rolling in, and he tumbles
   as well down the side of that van which resembles
      nothing so much as a forest dwarf's hutch on wheels

where he silently roars a great bouquet of flowers
    while his green and scaley winding tail anchors
        round the side window. Rose-white, a Unicorn

edged in icy blue rears opposite our flowerbreathing
    fire-eater now, its jewelous horn shining
        by moonlight, glowing

with a proud shy promise of goodness pure as silver.
    We cannot always be together,
        you and I, and I would have you remember

our fabulous creatures always—the bold Dragon
    as terrible as the horned horse is wonderful, twins of a wisdom
        older by far than we are in our kingdom

of daily things. Here, then, as a reminder, is the image
    of our Unicorn seen silver as he wades into waters ageless
        as the blue sky they reflect, hooves half tangled

in the world's common grasses. Keep him with you
    where you go and try from time to time gazing through
        your eyes as he gazes through his: *a sky beating slowly blue*

as the heart of all the air, grass burning green as an emerald's cooly imperial
and incessant stare, the inner brilliance of all that is natural
    held in that eye of his, which is every bit as real as he is invisible.

The Perfect Day

I wonder if you remember that summer, the Ashland
park a shimmering
Eden where iron gates could be forgotten,
grass stretching shrill along our thumbs,
eyes curious at the edge of a clearing,
and over pewter water the green willows of morning?

You lay curled on a bank, girl child
drowsing in a dandelion crown,
while I sat at a little distance
arrested by the perfect day.

When I saw swans bright as galleons
among the whitecap lilies
it did occur to wake you, but I watched you instead
while they drifted benignly on,
forgetting the disposition that goes with such grace.
Thus your first glimpse: the tumultuous
radiance of powerfully spreading
wings that rose up white from the wreckage of water
hissing through a golden beak and me
running toward you flapping my arms
helpless as the gates flung wide.

Window Built for My Daughter at Summer Solstice

1.
The window in the wall sits
square in wood cut square

by a circle toothed and turning.
Here the circle of the sun

shines through and the yellow
tooth and melon of the moon

shine through to your eyes.
And your eyes are the windows

of your skull, from which
your brain—nude hermit,

blind nun gazes out,
grateful for the view

and unaware of gratitude,
its graceful habit.

2.
Light pours into the window
bright or dim, shaping

all the space within
as fluids shape

to their containers: water
in the vase, air

in the expanding lung
gladness in the heart.

3.
Once the sun sets
and the moon,

all the nameless stars
whirl by. We look

out at them, name them
names we understand,

and they are constellations,
shapes given

by our need to know
what we cannot be known by.

4.
I turn to look
at you, daughter,

by the radiance
of dead stars

still lighting our earth,
and I see your face

gazing up and out
as I do now

into this darkness
generous with stars,

these points of light
by which men lost

in wilderness expanding
vast as time

permit themselves to dream
of their location.

5.
Every map at its edges
dissolves. We are

nowhere that would recognize
its name. The sky

turns round us
as we turn. I speak

the name we've given you
against the mystery,

and as your turn to me
the blaze of

what we know
could blind the sun.

Screen of Birds and Flowers
Written for my daughter's 12th birthday, accompanied by a small print

Opening and opening like this Chinese screen of birds and flowers,
the world, my daughter, tends year by year
to make an exquisite witness of the heart, which welcomes first
what's closest and most clear—that tree
filled with bright birds and brighter leaves,
this bush in all the stages of its blossoming—
before it favors giving over to the white voiced river
pouring down out of distant stone
as much a motion as a thing, an essence
into which you dip a hand
or plunge
shining, your whole body
a palm to scoop up light; later, what the mist obscures
will beckon, clarifying each impression, every
singing bird and gnarled stump that gave it perch,
and all the soaring blossoms
will ooze their scent again from the far shore
you have departed, following
the river out onto the ocean opening and opening before you.

Walking in Water Blue as Your Eyes

Months since that last trip to Banff
in my new Cadillac a year older than you,
gold as your hair in that foreign sun
we swam through, our fins elegantly
glinting through wilderness,
our clothes thrown off—yours neatly piled,
mine strewn—at every likely
curve of river hidden from the road.
Old Gold stood guard. We raced the dogs
across the rocks that made us skip and howl
then idled simple as otters
while they dozed, twitching in the sun.
Each night we lay by rivers under
stars wide-eyed as owls, spoke quietly,
woke comparing dreams, wishing for bacon.

All winter narrow snow
on the thin lines our talk ran through
constricted what we said in its long chill.
Now that the wires are bare and grass
interrupts the last patches of ice,
through our separation I can feel the sun
urging another summer. Old Gold
is out to pasture and Pup-Pup limps.
Glancing back through winter I see you
walking in water blue as your eyes.
The surface glazes when we leave
though the depths flow on. Soon, barefoot,
we'll give ourselves back twice
to the waters released for us—
once to reflect on it, once to get wet.

IV.   STRIKING   THE   DARK   AIR
FOR   MUSIC

"For Beauty's nothing
but beginning of Terror we're still just able to bear,
and why we adore it so is because it serenely
disdains to destroy us."

R. M. Rilke

I. Reckonings

I cannot find the dance
to rid me of this poison

[I Am Empty]

I am empty
given to a silence
I despise and need

I make nothing true

When I try to speak
without lies
nothing comes

I cannot bear the silence

My mouth
is a deep lie
crying out

My face a method
of deceit

My hands
lie cruelly
abrupt and graceless

So I hang from my bones
like rotten fruit, bleeding
and sweet
and only half covered by this swarm of words

[I Lie to My Friends]

I lie to my friends
for our comfort

My friends
Year by year they grow richer
these who started out so well

Now clusters of things
like platelets
in their veins
determine their lives

They marry
hate each other
hate hating
and the dying hatred is

They come to me
who am also richer
easier with things
and dying
of hatred and bored
with the dying

And they say to me
Isn't it nice
we still have the same tastes

[I Lie]

I lie. I lie by being
one body with one mouth
speaking from two lives, each
supporting, each
destroying one of me.

The blood of two men trying
to be born runs
crazed through my heart. My mind
tries to hold us together, tries
and fails.
            God in the darkness,
how we scream, each afraid
the other will hear how
close to death he's come, fearing
that other who comes through the dark
with shining eyes and the
last contract of mercy clenched
glittering in the dark.

In the silence of the night
we lie together, ghost
clinging ghost for warmth,
haunting this house of breath
with cries that do not come.

[My Lies Become]

My lies become
good pets, admitted
and pampered
by an old lady upstairs
in me. She stirs
from her rocking only
to refill their bowl
with dust urged
from her breast.
Then she'll lace with
crushed glass the bits
of meat made
of the newborn
and tossed at midnight
to the neighbors' beasts
—these she despises
for their size and ominous
good health.
                    Nightly
she reviews the subtle bodies
of her own and admires
their perfect grace as her
fingers curl and close
in the painful dark
that keeps her
as she would be kept.

She pulls the shades,
I close my eyes. We sleep,
giving the house entirely
to things that purr
and settle for the warmth
of our still body
and our breath.

[Why My Obsession with Lies]

Why my obsession with lies

If you could make it
worth my while
I'd take you to the ruins
you with your alien coins

Or maybe you believe I'm one
who fakes credentials, promises
exotic trips
but can't make it
home at night
without losing himself
in every sidestreet and open
mouth on the way

[If in a Strong Moment]

If in a strong moment
I admit to you
I have nothing to say
that is a lie

You know it

But why do you bother
with my miserable offspring
you with your own
scarcely tolerable lives

I cannot bear them
for you

Do what you must

[The Moon Set at Midnight]

The moon set at midnight
years ago
and still the houses on either side
glow with its dead light

There is nothing to rouse the dogs
and they sleep
in a glitter of dew
cold muzzles buried between paws

[Through This Glass Crowd]

Through this glass crowd
stars and the moon
to claim

me the table and page
on page unwritten there

real and dangerous
but nowhere
known yet—a void inarticulate

no way to say it
yet it
must be said

heavy cold hard
house of fire

the hand unable
to rouse
unable to please

the pressure
of stars incapable
of meaning

tongue a tin can
brain a box

hand an animal
fierce
hungering and empty

caught between two terminals:

stars beyond time
and the blood feeding now

[Up the Road Three Houses]

Up the road three houses
I made a friend.

His eyes are amber set
in raw hamburger.

I spend all day
touching him and talking.

His heavy mouth is inside out,
a meal he never finishes,

lips and tongue interrupted
by blunt teeth.

He smiles as I talk, I'm glad
he cannot help but smile.

I never feed him but at night
he comes smiling

and I hide until morning
when we talk in the new light.

[And All Night Long]

And all night long
sad laughter woke our wives

Friends
you must come again

Each Day, Each Night

I wait
in a house overlooking
a bay full of boats

and the strand
sinking and rising out
of the sea

impatient for something
to come
of haze in the morning

sun in the afternoon
then stars
and the moon

Various lights on the water

A Vice in Two Parts

I.
I'm the absurd chameleon, trying
to match the colors of the fire
    instead of leaping out.

II.
The madder I get the calmer I become
until I am a stone
    no one can throw.

[Dark Woods]

Dark woods. A dry
creek running
through dry trees.
Here no hawk can
break through
the loud thrash
of blown leaves
and the dry creek
draws no game
but me. I enter
bringing with me
into this sanctuary
of stunned trees
all the years of
hunger that make
my life a hunt.

[My Voice is Changing]

My voice is changing
I am changing too

with terrible impatience
that bursts

abruptly on the rocks
rising to shape

my course
with their impediment.

These I would dissolve in my
acceptance of them

if I could—

as a woman taking seed
makes of it

what her body will,
roots

that charge and drain
the altered stone.

[The Moon Like an Insect]

The moon like an insect
attracted by the room's light
presses to the window, clings.

Sometimes I am clumsy
with my wife when
she is helpless. But this

is not the moon's
affair: Why
should it threaten so?

It grinds against the
glass with its face
like diamonds, trying

to reach me.

[I Have Wakened to the Dark]

I have wakened to the dark
figure of a woman
coming down upon me

eyes wide
in her decomposing face
dead mouth opening

body opening to take
my body in
the seed I cannot hold

against the terrible
thrilling of her need

She turns away I wake
as from a dream
still vivid in the air

[First You Complain of Sleeplessness]

First you complain of sleeplessness
and then of dreams

I hear you out
know every cruelty
responsible

Like tin soldiers out trot
the professional
guardians of conscience: I am sorry

for your tears
when you cry out in the dark
turn to feel me there

turn and turn

[Suddenly Your Skull Shocks My Cheek]

Suddenly your skull shocks my cheek
with its grating attempt to kiss me
My lips tear flimsy as a child's kite between your teeth
I am a corpse in the third week of my death
startled by our manners
as we disembowel each other with the dry bones of our hands
each claiming something to remember the other by

Maybe Deception Is Truth's Odd Dimension

I.
I do not believe you

II.
You throw out words like clothes
and my limbs catch them—
coats for men with three arms,
sweaters without armholes.

I will not wear your lies.

I will walk in the grace
of my own perceptions, my body
trained to maneuver unthinkingly
in the lion's skin, my face
the owl's face.

III.
My vision is the vision of the hunter,
alert to the hidden fear in others.
I feed on you to maintain my great strength.
How can I love, I who hunger so,
whose blood will not be patient for your blood?

In the dark I move to tear away your soft words,
your warm clothes.
I move in disbelief straight to your heart.

[I Am Owl & Gull, Night & Day]

I am Owl & Gull, night & day.
Hungry in the dark & dangerous & joyful.
In the light a fisher, harmless brightwinged ghost crying
   one flat note of sorrow from its prison in the sun.

When the dark comes
my eyes darken for the new world & I set out on short strong wings
silent as the moon & stars riding with me in the sky
   & far below I see you
where you call for my soft questions
& the deep quench of my claws.

[I Take Quick Comfort]

I take quick comfort
in the glance of dew
the wide stare of the sea

but these things mean
nothing to me
that rouse up everything

A beast roused in its cage
torn on the bars
grinding its teeth on the lock

I cannot tell you

[Tonight No Moon]

Tonight no moon
but the
memory of your eyes in the dark
hollows of your face

[My Body Drifts, Atomic]

My body drifts, atomic
   cloud of stars lit
for one instant.
   Darkness is on every side
over and under me
   and as this cloud I am
is blown
   I become the dark
background for all beings, myself
   and not myself, having
stayed just long enough
   to see what's coming,
what has been
   and how I pass from
place to place, time
   after time.

[My Bones Are a Weapon]

My bones are a weapon
thrust into me
and into me, spreading
   from the first a formal alien support
      to uphold and shape me,
encasing in my brain
the slow disease of self.

Can I survive
these bones
I am made upon, left
   in me like the strange spears
      of the stranger enemy?
On this painless rack slowly
crazing with sorrows, I must live.

What a fabulous warfare
life is
as each man struggles
   through the stages of his being
      toward an end so utterly clear
that he interrupts his losses
only to praise them and pass them on.

[It's a Terrible Ease]

It's a terrible ease you have with your sorrows,
naming them names and arranging them to make sense of.
The syntax and cadence of grief: What is it?
You're the man handy with words,
a plumber of depths, you say,
but I wouldn't trust you with my pipes.
                              Wrenching
things around like that and screwing up your face
ought to come to something more than
these bills for failure. Receipts. Free admissions.

[Crickets]

Crickets.

*Quizzing
the dark? Singing?*

Scraping their knees.

*What good's that,
even for crickets?*

About as much good
as your question

or my answer,
or the light in this room.

Compared to the dark.

Without the scraping of knees.

[On My Wall]

On my wall there's a black and white blown
              up snap of an abandoned
warehouse on Cannery Row.
              A door torn wide open
on the third floor
opens from nowhere into nowhere
              and above the roof
above the opened door
a pigeon is frozen
              at the instant of ascent out of the dark.

The bird's like me
              sitting here telling
about it:
              It got its start and then was
stopped cold in the camera,

to appreciate the exact
              moment of release, held
forever near the original maw.
Except of course that real birds get away,
          wheeling
      free of all the films we can see.

[Enough Complaint]
Terza Rima in the manner of Mr. Berryman

Enough complaint. Enough
making of dead poems
in the presence of life.

It's spring and all the forms
of life brandish with silly
persistence their leaves, fronds,

buds and legs in an example he
dreads the promises of, threats
he will, he

says, live up to. (He'll take them by their throats
and drink till they inspire
him to follow their sappy examples.) What treats,

what near-visions he indulges, tires
of, runs from. He is fearful.
He brags, is shameful, would like to rear

like a white horse at the cliff's edge but instead will curl
around some soft words, warm
himself against them, hum, knit and purl

the raveling edges of his
life, ineptly dishonest, incapable of candor,
except in bed, where he fails, sometimes, even at this,

a downfall lacking
in the fine pierce of splendor.
And he is least a quack when he isn't quacking.

X/Y

X: You with your fine words
and signing my name to your poems.

Y: You always find a way out,
worming your fingers through my rib cage,
sticking my tongue out when the jawbone sleeps,
giving my seed into the prison of a woman's hips.
Just what is it you're up to, an exchange of hostages?

X: You, you are my clothes.

Y: Your poems would be sales slips
for purchases that can't be made.

X: Since when can the sleeve speak for the armpit?
My hands catch in your collarbones.
My legs dangle from the sudden spine
impaling my spirit. When your skeleton
started taking root inside me
I knew—I was hardening to death.

You call those changes "formal growth."

But I'm going beyond you.

I want out.

Hardscrabble

I.

Truces. Giving away
my claims to my life
in order
to have my life
permitted one more day.

Rain, rain, when you fall
the sun can shine,
not until.

    Storm, you gather in
    my heart.

II.

War, halfhearted you
will fail
to draw blood,
fail to heal. Insist
that each wound
be deeply revealed
to the sun, done with.

III.

Cowardice is crueler than any courage.
It wounds and runs away, dragging
apologies to cover all traces.
Back to the lair where it lies
all night, all day,
waiting for a lull
to strike again.

Catch it, beat it down!
Unwind it like a snake's length
from the anchor of its strength, its fantastic alibis.
Skin it out, then leave it to be cured
by its season in the open.

What remains that's worth life will rise up to the dance.

[I Live Now Day by Hour, by Glance and Breath]

I live now day by hour, by glance and breath
I am content
until the stars rise dragging out the dogs of darkness, my heart
    that bays across their tongues
challenging the stars
as their circles tighten overhead
and my spirit loosens from my bones to take the winds
    of the moon, joyfully deranging in this brilliance
that overwhelms the land of sleepers,
sealed and sane.

[Letters]

Letters. They've
served me
up to now. In them
I could talk
but the talk
was false and
killing me. Now
I write few
and send none.
Nothing I need
to tell can be
made fitting.
The moon and I
have a contract
the sun breaks
into. Grass
withers in its
fields at night.
In the morning
the dew ripens
like berries
in a young
woman's mouth
running and sweet.

Who could I tell?

Song Begging to Be Born

I.
No gentle birth, no
easy waking. Years
of my life I've
slept with only this
dream of the world
—that the world
was a dream. That
afraid. Paralyzed
into the poems where
I've nursed the
unacknowledged
passions of my life,
the cutting edge
of death moving surely
even through this dream.

II.
You're dying all around me.
You leave me
speaking this calm voice
that records, guts and preserves,
this voice I've dreamed excepts me
when there is no exception.

How can I wake and survive?
To wake now is to die
for the crime of wasting my life
in sleep, reasonable and calm.

III.
Wake me!— Wake me now
and to such pain I cannot speak
but must cry out cries so strong
from the roots of their anguish,
roots of their joy,
that my hungers sing!

2.   Songs from the Rim of the Wheel
Whose Center Is Everywhere

I cannot find the house
to hold me when I dance!

Song of the Last Hours

The last hours of the year and I am waking
through the slow cold avalanche of night among hills
and houses lost in the dark and glints of
stars uncovered in the rubble of trees and rooves and the pointed
ears of dogs alert to the dark
bodies among blind sheets turning
here in movements of sleep or movements of love or turning
at the same time slowly into the earth
among the unconscious dreams of the earthshaping
deep stones, thin seas, wider
insubstantial sky
apparent at all hours—Old skystone,
wheeling around the earth, held in its
circular sway, orbit
innocent of the record it is!

Song of Governance

Sometimes fading in the valley at dusk
I watch the high hawks in their circles shine
in the last sunlight, turning
and returning in the deadly orbits
of their craft, overhead
but below the stars and the governance
of their gradual circles.

Song in Five Parts

I.
I have been the planner
planned by another

far from me, far,
and me no longer.

The earth around me
turns within my mind

to salt. Its unspeakable
savors arrest me.

Looking backward, forward,
thinking, "There is no difference

between them—the present is
never with me."

Anchor me in this earth
that I may live,

whoever loves me!

II.
Moving, I love moving
through space

but time appalls me.
I grow dim, fade.

Praise God life's not
a highwire act: I am a bear

as clumsy off the ground
as I am strong among trees.

III.
Look backward, look forward,
what is there to see?

I lived once with my own fears
and my wife's

and I moved on. Moved on
but stopped

for one look back,
and froze.

Break me, for godsake
break me down!

Anger me with love now,
not with caution. Charity

is such a murder. Don't hang
back from me.

IV.
I have lived waiting for the blade
to fall.

I could not hide.
The blade was in myself.

Blade was myself.
Self fell: What bonds were cut?

What, whole and shining with strength,
will stride now from its prison

out into eternity?

V.
Here there are roses,
planted and tended

by the hands of men.
Berries in the hedges

cluster bright and red.
This is a new year.

I am a new man.
These are new tears.

Song of the Vines Ripening

For months the bare vines
winding through the trellis
have been hung with long dark pods
whose down caught
light from the sun and moon.

Today as I wrote you, puzzling
what to say, and how,
something clicked at my window.
I looked, no one was there.

Then
the window again. But this time
two brown beans shot through.
The pods—they were bursting, showering beans
to the earth
and the floor of my room.
                          Dried and shrunken
beyond bearing, they burst and flung out seeds like shouts of joy,
like these astonished words
I give you now.

Song of a Blind Traveller

As a blind man negotiates
rutted backroads, marvelling,
if he maintains his balance,
at his grace, so some men
leaning upon fences on the way
will amuse themselves
with the clumsiness they see,
while others, witnessing
his grace,
will share grace with him.

Song of Coordinates

I look out across clouds,
breathe thin simple air.

Whistle of a rockchuck.

Shadow of a hawk.

Hole in the earth.

Songs of Vanity: A Landscape of Voices

WATER
I am the water always,
clear and easy
for the creatures in me.
Never the same twice,
particle by particle I sink,
I rise. Always
the body of me stays.

I am the shining on the grass,
the twinkling of stars,
the ghosts from drowning fires,
tears, the brilliancy of eyes.
I answer thirst
or thirst has no answer.

Sky breathes me,
earth drinks me,
stones deny me
and I wear down stones.
Roots search for me,
I give myself to roots
and in that transport rise,
blossom and expire.

I feed you—I feed all life
streaming to the sea—
yet feed just upon myself.
I am with you at your birth,
attend you throughout life,
abandon you at death.

And I am water always.

LIGHT
You cannot see me
and I show you
everything you know.

I have no weight, no substance
yet
my effects are apparent everywhere.

I am constant,
various.

Too much of me
and you are blind
and too little
blind.

I am always on my way
beyond you, moving
as your bones beat once
farther than your numbers dream.

I am light.

AIR
I am the air.
Everywhere we
marry.

Every breath.

I am the child of light and water
passing through me
to themselves again.

I am vast and negligible,
scarcely there,
essential.

What I do not touch now
I have touched,
what I touch now
will be taken from me
and be back,

unearthed.
I am waiting.

Even to the grave I go
with the body,
whose gradual exhalation
frees me.

Take a deep breath,
hold it,
we
are becoming one.

POND
I am the pond, nothing
but other things
—water, air, the light.
I occur
when they meet here.

How can I speak
when I cannot imagine
I am real?—
I am a convention,
a crude one.

Define me with a measurement,
a volume,
brilliance, weight
—whatever means you wish—,
by the time you describe me
I am otherwise.

Springs increase me, freshen me.
The sun heats and robs me.
Creatures in me move,
the clouds on my surface shift,
I sink into the earth,
rise through the air.
Here one season,
in another, gone.

But if we do not worry so
with words,
you may enter into me with your whole being.

HERON
I am the heron.

I see you below me,
see you at a distance
in the tall grass,
watching.

You cannot approach me.
I am sensible and shy.
You're careless
with what you cannot use
—you cannot use me.

Among my own
life is a dire blessing,
simple, unreflective.
We join to court and breed,
play and fight, rear
our young and part.
We speak only to warn or summon,
to comfort.

We are silent.
We fish.

Yet I would starve
before I'd strike at the small fish
swimming there
in the reflection of your face.

Song of Emergency

After dreaming the pure pleasure
of a being loose in clear water,
diving easily in and out
of the warm mud deep at the bottom,
I wake to the risks of light.

I kick free and I streak
joyous as a bird toward the sun
out of the earth, through water, into the air
where I hang for an instant
free of awareness of safety, free of danger
in the dominion of the heron.

From this height
I glimpse at a distance, tall and white,
the still gods where they bend
above the pond or hunch in trees
to dry those wings spread glowing in the sun.
They stare into the shallows.
They shine like clouds.

At night I have slept dreaming
    of those reed-legged gods whose eyes are small suns,
who are silent
    but whose rare calls pierce my world like claws,
who fly as we dream of flying
    and burn against the sun in a great tumult of wings,
whose slow grace threatens us
    and woes us with its beauty,
who consume us to survive,
    whose lives we dread and envy.

Now I wait the moment when,
    suspended above the midworld of water,
I too will know the presence
    of the white cloud lowering,
the explosive sun quick
    above the pierce of the beak, the shrieking wings.

Song of Gifts

The first gift was hilarity as language vanished and my senses
were restored.

The second gift was the free place I knew wholly down to the
vibrance of the scales of each fish swimming the brook
through the valley of grasses.

The third gift was the hand darkness offered from darkness,
with the knowledge that holding the hand could comfort
and silence the moaning, but my efforts to pull it into
the light were violations of love with no success possible.

The fourth gift was the vision of my loved ones dead with age
and beyond me forever and the chance to ask my own
corpse a single question.

The fifth gift was fire: In that fire I burned
without even the promise of death to relieve my anguish.

The sixth gift was release from pain and access
to eternal energy.

The seventh gift was grace.

The last gift was re-entry into language and the loss of all
previous gifts into memory, for the final gift restored
my citizenship in Babel.

Song of Choice

silence
blessing
calling me when I am lost
                                        W. S. Merwin

I.
That man, standing there in the field,
his head hived with light
the colors of flowers,
his brain honeycombed with scent,
his tongue silent, tasting silence
—His presence is a marriage
with the earth and sky now,
each breathing moment
a treasury of delight.

II.
He cannot talk. Speech
betrays
everything precious he knows.
He tries, but he cannot talk.
Lies, all lies, speech
breeding sorrow if believed,
mistrust if not. What he has
is his because it is all
around him everywhere always.

III.
Speech divorces him from the earth.
Silence cuts him off from the human.
These, for a time, are the choices.

Song of When

O when I stood up walking
through the wall of light
and moved across the hill
down into the waterfall
what could my face say
to the visible glory of your face
and your eyes shining?

Grasses, Stones and Trees,
Sunshine and Cider,

—Hello, River!

I have moved
forever.

Song of the Bodynet

I am all appetite
a net flung to catch fish
        that catches stars

Song of Recognition

After the long letters
have been written, read,
abandoned, after
distances grow absolute
and speech, too,
is distance, only
listening is left.

I have heard the dark hearts
of the stones
that beat once in a lifetime.

Song of Presence

I let go of my darkness I have grieved there & been lost

I lay down in greenshining grasses smelling of them & rolling
    in them
I wake up in the dew where innumerable worlds orient & balance
    the sun recurring in each drop rounded by the light
    Earth rounded by our star's radiance
I wake up to the water wake up light wake dew grass & stones
    wake eyes & ears wake the pink cloud of my bones
    & old loves & new fulfill my spirit's waking

I wake up, Lord
I wake up to this blazing coat of joys
    no grief destroys

Song of Returnings

All the bones of the horses rise in moonlight
on the flatlands and hillsides, dropping
from trees, squeezing out from
under rocks, disengaging themselves
from the earth and things that live from the earth
and the scattered uniforms assemble
   to the sounds of bugling come back from the stars
and what has rotted into dust reforms with a furious sound
   of whirlwind tearing the faces from the astonished living
and gold flows molten from the mouth of Cortez
   and returns to the stones and the water and the air
and the redwoods collapse back into cones
and Christ is pried from the cross and flogged and spat upon
   and let loose among fishermen who scatter to their ships
   and enters his mother's womb and enters into the stars
and Babylon reassembles and Sodom and Gomorrah reassemble
and David sings then babbles in his mother's arms
and all living things return to their sources
and the waters return to their sources
and the sun returns to the source
and the vast darkness returns
and all things are
and are not.

Song of Shedding Light and Darkness

Stars
     stars
  and grass deepening
the dark fields

No one
     walks here
  with me and I feel
the hillside moving

as I move
     enclosed
     by stars, abrasive
and careless, turning

around me
     grinding
     light and the darkness
from my skin, skin

from my
     bones until
  blind and clean
I am ready to go on

Song of What the Rain Said

Rain speaks to the grass.

I overhear it
and my ears get wet.

Song of Benediction

May light sweeten in your lungs
may your tongue shine

May you be grateful to your body
   for the offenses it forgives you
may your body please you
may your mind accept its forms
   and guide you among dangers and pleasures

May you love yourself as you are loved

V.   L O V E   P O E M S

"deep-grooved for living feet by ancient hooves"

Ways Water Has

It always moves and pleases me, these ways
the ocean has with walls of adamant—urgent and lavish,
restless as the moon, persistent as darkness;
even the lesser wave as it meets stone
breaks into brilliance
and that fluent whisper riotous in the graceful rush of foam.

And look,
see how these reefs admit and shed what washes over them,
resisting and absorbing, in one stance, the myriad approaches
        of the sea,
and how carelessly the simple water fondles, shocks
and undermines the fundamental granite
touch by touch.

That innocent reduction of the upright cliff
to puffs and swirls of dust
the wingbeat of the least seabird can scatter!

May I know a woman who has known the sea.

The Shining Everywhere
     for Ivy Becher

The sun you face in Texas,
near the Mexico border,
reflects from your eyes
green as shallow water
over sand, over stone,

and is guided onto canvas
into horses and flowers
or faces and the shapes
of trees you've never seen
except in imagination,

and that same sun faces me
here in Montana, glares
from melting snow on trees
you've never known, flares
into rainbow where the air

is right for it and appears
to head each day for
the valley to the west
as a child tumbles dimly
for the same pillow

night after night. What tree
where you live does the sun
nest in each afternoon
before it sleeps and falls
over the edge of Earth?

Falling in its dream it must
open like a white flower
over China, over India
and Asia, Athens, Rome
and Barcelona, where

the sleepers wake and rise
into their lives
as we soon wake and rise
—dewbright feet still chilled
from brilliant fields of sleep—

in Brownsville and Missoula,
you to paint, I to write
in the bright and binding grace
of this singular sun that keeps us
and keeps our loved ones shining everywhere.

From the Other Shore
for my mother, my daughter, my sisters

Waiting to be served we look from the veranda
down into a river
   whose unpronounceable name
would mean nothing to you. Thick
green trees on the opposite bank ignite
as an elongated sun
   touches their fringes,
and sheep gathered there to drink
slowly retreat into shadows
where their suncharged fleeces
   still glow in the dark.

Much farther downstream,
   beyond where its broad back carries clouds,
some of the black rocks
   gathered at a bend
are in motion, rise and
fall, rising again
   and again as we
see, our eyes now focussed
for the distance,
   the lengths of brightness
each rock flails, causing
the other, dormant stones
   to shine.

Washerwomen. Probably
wives and mothers
   to the shepherds
we sense watching us
from the other shore. Perhaps

the white shirts
    of the waiters brighten
drubbed upon those stones.
By the time the meal
    is served and removed
in a flaring of silver
from these tablecloths
    immaculate in late
sunlight, we can hear
faintly the dull reports
    of wet clothes slung
heavily down upon the stones.

First the flash and only
moments after the *slap*
    slap these flat stones
have known for centuries
or more, before learning
the roar of cars like ours,
    casually laden
with items worth
more than we had known
    before we saw the
stones of the river rising up
in the forms of women.

                    —Yugoslavia—

Dancers on an Island with No Roads

Taverna on an island with no roads
but donkey paths. Along these ruts flowers
break from stones as overhead
the sun, moon, clouds and stars take turns
against the darkness where he walks
cold, broke, and happy with his life.

"Excuse me—do you speak English?"
He nods, glancing up from the cloud
of ouzo into the face of a Chicago
seamstress, one of the new tourists
he saw jounce by on burros at noon.
"Are you one of the dancers?"
                He laughs,
wishing he were, here where the waiters,
grave in their white shirts and black slacks,
still give themselves as passionately to
bazouki and balalaika as to tips. "No, no,
American," he confesses. "Like you."

Later, in a darkness rendered delicate
by the pale walls and flowering almonds
of the patio his small room opens to,
his landlady—haggard, wrapped
in black and outrage,
hands and face moonflashing as she
flails him with her broom
and points a crooked fingerbone
at the grinning seamtress—shrieks
again and again: *No no American!*

All night along the path above the sea
goats grazing silver hillsides hear them laughing,
their way lit by sunflowers below the moon
where they dance among dark stones
deep-grooved for living feet by ancient hooves.

               —Hydra—

Sketches of a Woman in Various Attitudes

1.
A dim pillow lumped
before my eyes
brightens
as your face rises

and all of the horizon

warms as my free hand
like an antelope at dawn
sets off across the ridge
of what you are beside me.

2.
Owl to my owl tree,
hooting and who-ing,
raven
ravenous as I am,

heron longlegged on
the level shore, striding
among the green pads
of plain dailiness,

you brighten up
the mud
with these reflections
of your grace.

3.
Your pale hands glowing green
in the uppermost leaves
    of your garden
drift among the last blossoms
like geese among the first
    shale-edged winter winds,
wedges of late light against the night sky.

4.
Your face rising
like the desert moon

above the pale tarantula
of my shoulder

as I shave

has caused me to learn
the delicate art

of carving
around a smile.

Rain, You Say

Rain, you say, rain falling
among the plum and cherry
trees whose fruits we shared
this summer walking where
they fell to the sidewalks,
rolled into the streets.
Those same streets,
if they would,
could flow together now
leading me over the highest
passes glistening with snow
and on beside the three rivers
home to your door.
                    Where I am
it is snow falling and columns
of shocked mercury falling
below zero, fixing all

the trees and houses,
all the hills and hollows
in a lunar nimbus
bright and frail yet capable
of shearing sheets of stone
from cliffs like stiff pages
turned in an old book.
Come spring and thawing rains
and all this hardened surface
shifts, slips into the foam
of streams like broken mirrors
I will follow shining
home to you.
                    Rain, you say.
Rain falling. Soon.

Love Poem

1. The last sounds before sleeping
are the first birds of morning
and your breathing.
—How I dream!

2.
No stone so deep in Earth
as I in you
nor cloud so moved by wind
as I, by your warm hand.

Exchanging Glances

I stand on the porch
of your second floor apartment, drinking in
the breeze through my loosened shirt and holding
cold beer to my mouth. You are inside bathing
by the window open over the garden, preparing
to be loved. Two weeks gone
is long enough to sweeten our reunion as the bitterness
of beer is sweetened by the chill. At the *slap slap*
of your bare feet approaching from behind
I slip off my sandals, loosen
the sweaty belt in my pants and see, suddenly,
below me, peering up through branches,
a small boy, face open as a small bird's mouth.

As we exchange that glance
I see again the huge man guzzling beer and leaning
on the flakey white railing overhead, his shirt sweaty and loose
to the summer heat and his pants half open as he
leans over, looking down
into my startled face: *He's*
going to piss on me I think, freezing
to the spot as he smiles down, salutes me with his beer
and turns to go inside. Raising my empty bottle
to the boy, I smile the promise down to him and turn back into
my own life, your life,
our life as it is now

Fleshflower

1.

There is one flower,
one blossom,
exotic and common,
blooming only in the dark
despite sunlight and moonlight.

Despite starlight and streetlight
it blooms
    only in darkness
and is blooming everywhere
around us, always.

Unblinking.

2.

It is the flower of electric muscle
darkrimmed, half concealed,
    and at the hollow core
pink as sunrise, a white rabbit's eyes. Closeup

it can be opened as a honeyburdened
blossom, by tongue,
by fingertip,
by the right words sung at the right pitch.

Closeup you see that it is blind, is
slowly weeping. It trusts
    simply the genius
        native to those complex roots

extending outward to the stars and
in toward each cell's center
to determine,
Is this friend or foe prying
the leaves

apart, trying

some kind of entry, some
visitation?

3.
   If the ground
the plant is bedded in
entirely approves the care
afforded by your gardening hands,
if you tender it with gentleness
enough, with strength enough
and of the right kind,

and with songs vibrant as the
humming of the bee is
to the blind heart of its most random choosing
in the world that blossoms
only at its and at the wind's
wandering but insistent touch,

it will take you in
to the radiant secret chamber,
it will set beating your wild secret heart
in its good time, and yours.

It will accord you morning and evening glory.

It will cause you a sweet crown of joy.

4.
In a tongue not ours
but human as we are human
there is a written character
which makes three names:

Call it *Tulip*, you will name it truly.

Call it *Cunt*, you speak the second name.

Or let truth have its home

for a moment on your tongue,
and utter it in praise

for the last name is called *Gates of Paradise.*

In a Natural Place

1.
We step carefully,
naked among rocks

invisible in
claycolor water,

and feel the current
sucking us

as sunlight sheers
past the cliff

to lay upon us
a second skin

of healthy brilliance.

2.
Just this—

nakedness
in a natural place

and laughter. How
good it feels again

to be this close
with you in a space

so expansive
the earth we walk

seems like the
miracle, with

all this flowing
around our feet

and glistening calves
its special blessing.

3.
Stumbling, brushing fingertips,
we pick our way

carefully, our hearts
gradually careless again

as we lie down
stretching out

in the chill stream
and shining light

to tell
what the rush

of light past
our floating faces

draws from us,
the dreams this

living water releases.

4.
How I

wanted you then,
woman,

your hair and skin
gleaming tawny

in my eyes, your eyes
opening blue

into wide air
where I would soar

like the hawk
our laughter earlier

started into
flight

from its branch
of hunger. Remember

how it lifted off
and rose, its grace

stripping all noises
from our tongues?

5.
But this was long ago,
so far away that now

the sun setting in my eyes
rises in yours.

Even so, at night
when sleeping

scours me of old doubts,
I know a being

hovers over both of us
higher than that hawk

and gloriously shining
as we turn like stones

rolling in the water
of each other's absence,

our fears no more or less
than the deep fall of shadows

our bodies
render luminous.

6.
That hawkhigh eye of light,
the sun, still waits

for us to waken
into skins brilliantly

fitted for desire.
Our canyon

is still there,
that stream. Those stones

worn smooth and round
by a vast patience.

—Aravaipa—

Leveling

Because I miss your hands,
as delicate and shy
and difficult to touch
as quick fish that glide
glittering like dreams
in their other world,
and miss them, still,
so much, my slippery
absence, my bright twin,
I have begun
praying that my hands
be made again
and made of water
that need not clutch
to hold, nor hold
to know.

VI. CREATURES

That within us
is without.

Slugs Amorous in the Air

"The spirit moves,
Yet stays:

...

A small thing,
Singing."

Theodore Roethke

On mucous films they glide,
gracefully monstrous:

slick misbegotten whales,
halved, cast out onto land,

shrunken, left to cross forever
the shoreless sea of earth.

Indifferent to us,
these constant voyagers

detecting in each other clues
of readiness—who knows how?

They soar like gradual
eagles up a bank of tree

out onto a dark current
of limb, then dangle

from a single length
of shared umbilicus

high in clear blue
air, spinning

slowly in the globe
of their own motion,

two beings intent
upon each other

as only lovers are,
each laved by the liquid other

in bodylength embrace.
Like darkly pairing tongues

or the sundered halves
of Leviathan

trying bright reunion
in their sea of air,

they hang in that whole kiss
while we look on

radiant with disgust and envious,
pitching toward awe

as from each head
organs emerge unfurling

like silk parachutes
exquisite with awareness,

each coddling its exact
other in the counterfeit

with a long careful touching,
numinous as saints,

unutterably lewd
as they merge

in a bright soft lock
joined as orchids

might join if animated
by desire, trembling

blossom against blossom,
slow pulse

matching slow pulse
as these doubly sexed

beings will do,
continuing an hour

and more,
each gross shape further

extending (from the chill
of what should be

its head) the lucent
figure of an organ

wholly sexual as angels,
male and female brilliance twinned.

And what passes
between them

in this urgent healing
sought by the never whole

passes slow as nectar
shining in the deepest

flower we know
and multiplies

into these glistening miracles
we who grow gardens

in our annoyance
never guess.

Answering Dance

Dark abdomen upraised,
pulsing and pulsing,
she signals from
the heart of the web.
He drops everything
to join her,
nimbling through the maze
of stalks and stems
that bramble between him
and the polestar
of his desire.

At web's edge
he pauses, eyes
kaleidoscopic
in the hood of his head.
Alert to any sign
excited in her,
he tenses and waits,
carefully strumming
on one string, importantly
distinguished
from stray fly or bee
by his request.

Her answering dance
invites him on.

Entering her domain
he is entranced
by the spell
all around her of fine lines
and the silkbound husks
staggered at random
among them

and by the global dew
in which worlds
reverse and shine
that will vanish
at the brush
of a leg.

They greet,
an intimate complex
of touches, taps
and nudges as leg
brushes leg after
leg. He mounts her,
shudders, mounts
again, and again
the trembling web
scatters its dew.

She grows arch
and still. He
flickers
with exhaustion
beside her, thrums
the single string
and waits, bouyant web
resonant with his appeal.

Allowed to pass,
he vanishes
into the tall grass;
but if he carelessly
alarms her, strikes
one alien note,
stunned by her solution
he is spun into a state
ancient as night
and deep as the hunger
yet to come
of dark sons and daughters.

The Jellyfish

There isn't much a man can do
about a grounded jellyfish
except step over it, or prod
it with his walking stick, and if
he has no walking stick, his shoe.
My feet were bare, so I leaned
to watch the waves relax around
the shiny melted-looking heap.

The jellyfish didn't move,
but then, of course,
jellyfishes don't.
They navigate at best
like bottles: When the tide shifts
they bob and drift away. But who
has ever seen a living creature
with a note inside?
                        I found
an iridescent fish, undigested,
twitching still inside the gluey
drying bowel. I saw it jerk,
expand its gills, then quiver,
arrested loosely, loosely and forever.
It shone with pink and green, blue
and yellow, flashed profoundly silver
in each spasm. I knew it was dead
already, and only seemed to work
to free itself.
                    As I tried to remove
the notion from my mind, the mound
it moved in, like a glassy brain,
was taken from me by a wave
that slid from the ocean without a sound.

Arctic
for Robert Hedin

From its polished display case
this one stares back at us,
almost contemptuous.

Dead claws hooked
in the lifelike branch,
its beak is half parted
as if to remark
on the brass
of the nameplate
where Greco-Latin nominations
encase him in another
kind of glass
to be held back by,
beheld in.
         No wind
will alert him
of our presence.
No snapped branch
set him
soaring like a moon
among glazed clouds.
Nor will the museum's
rats tempt him
in the dark
to hunch and spread
his wings and tail and fall
silent as moonlight
upon the quick hot
frenzy in that fur.

Nor in fact could anything be said
to move him now.
This is what we learn
from him, if
we learn at all: That he
is dead, stuffed

among the mystery
of all that has been.
Is changed as we
are changed,
gazing upon him.

Moon-eyed Owl,
for whom the night is eyes,
Cloud-voiced Owl,
charged by the intelligence
of snow to utter brilliance,
it is you, Lightning-taloned,
you of the Arrow-tongue,
you alone who know to summon
from the live red flesh that breath
bright as dew called from grasses by the sun.

And it is you, Whose-Feathers-Whisper,
you of whom it is known
that we will
hear him
one day, or one night,
hear him call our name
in a language of light
that must illuminate us
each in the locked museum
of all we thought
we knew and, having heard,
we will rise up
nearer to his voice
on our unfathomable wings
to ask who he was calling for, who? Who?

Elegy for Apu

for Sharon

Apu ben Gasser, Afghan hound
And gentleman, court jester in repose
But clearly a king once he rose
To stretch or circle in the room, round
And round, until his chosen plot
Of rug was freed of snakes, the grass
Of his imagination tramped flat
As he could make it with his great black feet,

And Apu running, covering the long green ground
As if grace made his body its pure dance
Of speed and beauty, muscles flowing over bone
Concealed beneath deep fur, his elegance
Like water smoothly flexing over stone,

And Apu, who, for his mistress,
Strode across the fields of show and
Stately, at his ease,
Held firm under the judge's hand:

Apu—clown, king, champion,
Gentleman, and friend—

Apu is dead.

Salmondream

for Judith Anne Azrael

Salmon in the river blur
like dreams, then reappear
to break the surface
with disturbances healing
at the speed of light.

We watch, intent, blind
to the clouds and leaves
swimming the wind. By chance
I watched a forked twig running
at the speed of water

pass over the falls and the falls
freeze into focus: A salmon
springs from froth
solid as snow. Each scale is clear
and our universe, inverted in that eye,

shines as far and brilliant as the moon.
You are there and I am there, all of this,
caught forever in the alien lens
of an eye staring from the face
assumed by water. Seen and gone.

Kiiiiiii

for Jim Heynen & Ray Carver

From the high blue sunspoked wheel of pure dispassion
    an eagle tumbles
as one fish through the deep green shadow rises, brightening,
and where these arcs concur
      claws seize
and silver skin erupts
a sudden jewelry of shuddering.

Wind from the great wingbeats flattens the water.

The salmon arches and sips through delicate gills
    the first deep shock of
air, locks, its fixed gaze clouding in the thinning waters,
blind to the steadily
      rowing
    figure of their shadow.
Above curve twin suns darkly glittering.

VII. INVISIBLE GUESTS

"I am like a room with innumerable fantastic mirrors
that distort by false reflections one single pre-existing reality
which is not there in any of them
and is there in them all."

—Fernando Pessoa—

"The purpose of poetry is to remind us
how difficult it is to remain just one person,
for our house is open, there are no keys in the doors,
and invisible guests come in and out at will."

—Czeslaw Milosz—

1.   "These Are The Children"

"By Their Own Truthful Masters"

The following, writes Charles Dickens, *are a few
specimens of the advertisements in the public papers.
It is only four years since the oldest among them appeared;
and others of the same nature continue to be published
every day in shoals.*

from *AMERICAN NOTES, 1842*

Ran away, Negress Caroline.
    Had on a collar with one prong turned down.
Ran away, the negro Manuel.
    Much marked with irons.
Ran away, a black woman, Betsy.
    Had an iron bar on her right leg.
Ran away, the negress Fanny.
    Had on an iron band about her neck.
$100 reward, for a negro fellow, Pompey, 40 years old.
    He is branded on the left jaw.
Ran away, a negro boy about 12 years old.
    Had round his neck a chain dog-collar
    with "De Lampert" engraved on it.
Ran away, the negro Hown.
    Has a ring of iron on his left foot.
Also, Grise, his wife,
    having a ring and chain on the left leg.
Ran away, a negro boy named James.
    Said boy was ironed when he left me.
Committed to jail, a man who calls his name John.
    He has a clog of iron on his right foot
    which will weigh four or five pounds.
Detained at the police jail, the negro wench Myra.
    Has several marks of LASHING,
    and has irons on her feet.
Ran away, a negro woman and two children.
    A few days before she went off, I burnt her face.
    I tried to make the letter M.
Ran away, a negro man named Henry,
    his left eye out, some scars from a dirk

on and under his left arm
and much scarred with the whip.
Committed to jail, a negro man.
  Has no toes on the left foot.
Ran away, a negro woman named Rachel.
  Has lost all her toes except the large one.
Ran away, Sam.
  He was shot a short time since through the hand,
  and has several shots
  in his left arm and side.
Ran away, my negro man Dennis.
  Said negro has been shot in the left arm
  between shoulder and elbow,
  which has paralyzed the left hand.
Ran away, my negro man named Simon.
  He has been shot badly,
  in his back and right arm.
$25 reward for my man Isaac.
  He has a scar on his forehead,
  caused by a blow; and one on his back,
  made by a shot from a pistol.
Ran away, a negro girl called Mary.
  Has a small scar over her left eye,
  a good many teeth missing, the letter A
  is branded on her cheek and forehead.
Ran away, negro Ben.
  Has a scar on his right hand;
  his thumb and forefinger being injured by being
  shot last fall. A part of the bone came out.
  He has also one or two large scars on his back and hips.
Detained at the jail, a mulatto, named Tom.
  Has a scar on the right cheek, and appears to have been
  burned with powder on the face.
Ran away, a negro man named Ned.
  Three of his fingers are drawn into
  the palm of his hand by a cut.
  Has a scar on the back of his neck,
  nearly half round, done by a knife.

Was committed to jail, a negro man.
> Say his name is Josiah.
> His back very much scarred by the whip;
> and branded on the thigh and hips
> in three or four places, thus (JM).
> The rim of his right ear bit or cut off.

$50 reward, for my fellow Edward.
> He has a scar on the corner of his mouth,
> two cuts on and under his arm,
> and the letter E on his arm.

Ran away, from the plantation of James Surgette,
> the following negroes: Randall, has one ear cropped;
> > Bob, has lost one eye;
> > Kentucky Tom, has one jaw broken.

Ran away, Anthony.
> One of his ears cut off,
> his left hand cut with an axe.

$50 reward for the negro Jim Blake.
> Has a piece cut out of each ear, and the
> middle finger of the left hand
> cut off to the second joint.

Ran away, the Mulatto wench Mary.
> Has on the left arm a cut,
> on the left shoulder a scar,
> two upper teeth missing.

Ran away, my man Fountain.
> Has holes in his ears, a scar
> on the right side of his forehead,
> has been shot in the hind parts of his legs,
> and is marked on the back with the whip.

Brought to jail, John.
> Left ear cropt.

$250 reward for my negro man Jim.
> He is much marked with shot in his right thigh.
> The shot entered on the outside, half-way
> between the hip and knee joints.

Ran away, a black girl named Mary.
> Has a scar on her cheek, and the end
> of one of her toes cut off.

Taken up, a negro man.
> Is very much scarred about the face and body,

and has the left ear bit off.
Ran away, my negro man, Levi.
　　His left hand has been burnt, and I think
　　the end of his forefinger is off.
$25 reward for my man John.
　　The tip of his nose is bit off.
Ran away, Jose Dennis.
　　Has a small notch in one of his ears.
$25 reward for the negro slave Sally.
　　Walks as though crippled in the back.
Ran away, negro boy, Jack.
　　Has a small crop out of his left ear.
Ran away, a negro man named WASHINGTON.
　　Has lost a part of his middle finger,
　　and the end of his little finger.
Ran away, a negro man, named Ivory.
　　Has a small piece cut out of the top of each ear.
Ran away, a negro woman named Maria.
　　Has a scar on one side of her cheek, by a cut.
　　Some scars on her back.
Ran away, a black woman, Betsy.
　　Had on her right leg an iron bar.
Ran away, a negro named Arthur.
　　Has a considerable scar across
　　his breast and each arm, made by a knife;
　　loves to talk much of the goodness of God.

Burning

for Richard Thomas

I was no one
until they made me
afraid

Made me something fearful

Until they made me have
to survive them

Now I have deeply plunged
my hands
bleeding through the dark
broken windows of their streets

I've watched them
I've learned

I've seen them breaking in
to my people
breaking in to the faces of children
leaving nothing but nigger grins

Breaking in to our lives
our women
leaving us to lie
about ourselves

Leaving us ruins

With my best nigger grin
I take their curse
I take it
I give it back burning

So I have let the old bright
currency of their being

run freely through my fingers
flowing
warmer than anything
even my women can offer me

And Lord I am changing

Lord I am consumed by change
now that I have seen myself
caving in
in windows caving in
and seen myself flickering
in fragments
on the streets

Now that I have seen myself
my whole world
burning

Curse of a Good Citizen

They are poisoning
the air and the water
I must daily
breathe and drink

I watch my family
breathe and drink
the poisons they are
told they breathe and drink

They feed the winter streets
with salt
I feed my car and shoes
to the salt.

They ask for my son
so I give him
to be trained for their purposes
to be taken away

They block my windows
with buildings
then offer the moon
live on TV

They hide the country
behind billboards
urging me
to move to the country

They cut down the forests
surrounding the city
I have made my home
with their foods

They force me to work in their unions
then force me to strike
They raise my wages
then raise the prices

They wire that my son is dead
and wire the money
for burial
I bury him with their money

They urge me to vote
and I vote

They tax me
I give them my money

I curse them on each of these counts
and on others

They accurately record my complaints

Silhouettes

In one of the nation's culture-minded cities
—and quite likely in several dozen more—
wait semi-transients some prole angel pities,
who gather every morning by the score
in a union hiring hall. Against the wall
where cracked plaster discloses the mean ribs
of lath, they sit on benches. The papers call
these separate men "the labor pool that gives
our state potential."
        Slouched, they wait and read
the latest news. "The war'll help," says one.
When the others grumble, he shakes his head.
"True's true," he says, and stares.... Against the sun-
lit skylight, relic from the building's past,
the rain-dropped tadpoles are still, sperm-like, and black.

Malfunctions

"At my age, an unimportant spasm.
The heart's a sturdy organ, very strong.
They tell me it's no more than that,

"and who am I to argue? I'm not fat,
not nervous. I'm used to working all day long.
At my age, an unimportant spasm

"—dizziness, momentary lapses.
They know their diagnosis can be wrong.
They tell me it's no more than that

"'malfunction,' the skipped beat. A fact
to know but not to worry over. Not for long.
At any age, an unimportant spasm

"—dwelt on— can precipitate attack.
The heart's a sturdy organ, very strong
they tell me. It's no more than that:

"Strong and sturdy, leaking like a sack.
Each beat more life gone.
At my age, an unimportant spasm.
To tell me it's no more than that!"

Lunch Hour

Behind a department store
whose glassy face displays on Market Street,
a one-way alley stretches
a block at a time through the city. Out of sight
and mind, with butts and wine,
it's here the morning drunks slump as papers
blown from refuse boxes
scrape along the asphalt, stiff as crabs.

Because it's quieter here
in the corridor of red brick walls
like cliffs, I sometimes eat
propped against a knobby fire-plug's stump
on the curb, killing time.
The men around watch as I wad up the sack,
toss it onto the street.
While it crawls along in the wind, I sit with the others
empty-handed. Hunched
like men at a beach, we listen and watch. We wait.

Stockroom
Early in the fall

The stockroom fills with clocks at noon
—thank God they don't come wound. Until
my time has come, I'll work balloons,
I'll sort deflated faces. Tell
me what they'll mean—a child's puffing
swollen face, his tears, a mother's
breath, his joy, another thing
the wind can pop on thorns, another
thing? I'll sort and count and stack
or hang brassieres and blouses, trusses,
knee-length socks, keeping track
of tennis rackets while the busses
murmur past nine floors
down.
       Once I dropped and broke
a bottle of cologne. Whores,
genie-like, appeared from smoke
no eye could see, no nose ignore.
Dizzily I kneeled to dam
the spreading stain with rags. "More
pantie girdles," wheezed the man
from lingerie. "But these are all
there are," I said, pointing beyond
the toys, cosmetics and dresses for fall
to garments stacked on the pricer's bench.
They glistened like skinned fish.
He winced and, turning from my stench,
he moaned, "There must be more than this,
there must be more than this."
           At noon,
poised on the window's tilting ledge I ate
my lunch, repeating with the cadence
of a clock's neat tick:
There must   there must   be more   than this.

Estrangements

A man and his wife are estranged.

They have a child
they love.

The child returns from a visit
with the father
carrying a sack of candy
the mother sees and takes
and throws away.

The child cries, the mother cries,
the father, if he knew,
would cry.

The father knows.
His wife has told him
of that illness, often.
How the hands chill,
the eyes glaze.

But the father loves the child
and the child loves the father.
Neither has a full knowledge of love
and there are things
to be put in love's place.

So the child cries, the mother cries,
and the father, if he knew,
would cry.

Death of a Family

The feral boys swinging in Sunday suits
can scarcely be distinguished
from the grey branches they seize,
rattling them to fling the pecans down.

Anxious as squirrels among the leaves
their fathers are below, gathering what falls.
The failing patriarch abhors them all,
but, rasping, orders them to stay.

At twilight in that wasting house,
the women—intimidated by relief,
regret, and willful love—surround him,
storied eyes imploring, fervid with decay.

Above them all, below them,
moonlight and dry frozen roots spread
and clutch, contending for a world beyond
the coins and curtains of his tended sleep.

The Grandfather
At a family picnic

From wave to wave a flat rock skips,
skids. An edge catches. It flips and sinks.
Each time he throws, the watch in his pocket clinks

on the coins and collected pebbles. How many trips
he's made back here, to pry stones from the chinks.
   From wave to wave each flat rock skips,
   skids till it catches an edge, flips, and sinks.

His wife complains, insists that his pocket rips
from carrying "sharp, dirty stones." She thinks
aloud, "He's my oldest child." Their grandson blinks.
   From wave to wave the flat rock skips,
   skids. When it catches its edge, flips and sinks,
   the water twinkles. He flinches. The watch in his pocket clinks.

August at Sixty
   for Gail

She stands alone now, widowed in their garden
with the comfort of his roses
hung from ruined stems.
The mannered children, who were kind, are gone,
resuming lives remote from hers again.

She plucks off yellow leaves and ties up stalks
the dry weather has weakened.
Her apron fills with leaves.
stiff fingers brush her belly, breasts and hair,
trembling with this new life she must bear.

Ceremony

Deep in the calm of a drawing room of flowers
the only hand her father holds
is dead.

       Years ago,
behind a locked and broken bathroom door,
they found a man with eyes of dull blue silk
hanging from a tie stretched thin and knotted
in his puckered throat. She felt her father's love
as, in a shock of tenderness, his hand quickened
her arm and, loosened, dropped away. She left
them kneeling, one still, one slowly
turning, head cocked, hands loosely bound
and naked in a small bright room—her father
in the slowly turning shadow of his son.

She sits apart, alone
in the alcove reserved for close relations.
Staring through the arch that frames
her mother's face and brother's
in her memory, she knows that if her father sees
he sees her framed in that same arch of flowers,
watching, heart and buttocks clenched
as at his touch.
       Among the heads before her
she sees a former suitor's dull profile,
his wife, her father's business partner
and a friend, then half a dozen friends,
a row of strangers who look up to turn away.
She knows the faces dark with memories
she cannot know, and watches each face
patterned by the shadow of its neighbor,
watches features vanish, then reappear as restlessness
shifts a wife or husband, or a stranger
turns to stare and look away.
       He is gone now,
he is gone, and who are you to sit prim
among roses and lilies, breathing

this sweet stench of bright dead flowers,
breathing? Now he's gone: Without him,
who are you? Breathing among roses,
half-opened and dead, breathing
among lilies and roses, who are you?

                              he is gone now
he is gone   please now   he is gone
the grass is soft   and look   the house
is empty   we're alone now   please
                              the grass is soft
the grass is soft and
                    he is gone now
please the grass is soft your breasts
are white and
                    soft with hands and
please the grass is
                    blue eyes
please
        dull blue
                please
                    Please

                              "Please!" she cries,
then sees them turn to stare. The blank profile
starts to rise, a stranger, a frightened face
that says familiar words. On everyone
a neighbor's shadow falls.

                              Outside
the sun is green in summer leaves and grass.
She sees his boy, a face pressed to the glass,
as he stares from the car at their approach.
They enter, sit in silence, and watch
the child run to his mother. Passing
cars flash the sun's sharp light
against their faces.

                    "Are you all right?"
he asks. She nods an answer,
takes the hand he gives,
then lets him lead her to the waiting grave.

Oldtimers

for Hank Felstad

I grab my sump-pump
by the hose and drop
the deadweight down
into the dark
below the deck,
take a last look
at blue sky,
then follow down
a steel ladder
welded to the slick
bilge wall. Hit
bottom ankle-deep
in sludge, then
through a dark hole
opening through darkness
drop it down again,
again.

The dead air
of the darkness chugs.
Racket of a heart
sucking up mud,
sucking and rocking.
I try breathing
through my sleeves
but give it up.
Try whistling
but the pump drowns
whistling out.
Try singing next. Then
riveters begin working
the hull by my head.
My brittle teeth chatter
like bright rivets.

Those lucky monkeys hung
out there in sunshine,

eyes clenched in blank goggles
while the rigid mouths grin.
You blast a hull like
that all day—nothing
between you and nothing
but the plank you plant
your sweet ass on—
friend, you pay off
debts no store on earth
would recognize.
To reach me here
the natural light
would have to wind
down sixty feet,
then search.

Next level down
three black guys
on their hands and knees
swab it up with rags.
When one rears back
to strike a match
I can see the others'
teeth blinking
in the dark. It means
they're singing. They're
old timers. They
don't have to hear
it to sing it
anymore.

—Todd Shipyard, Seattle—

The Last Days of a Retiring Executive
for Wally S.

It started with my notice three weeks back. How could I
   not have been aware before of the gradual pleurisy of
   spirit in their faces red-eyed and sniffling, aware
   of their faces as hopelessly flat as the quarterly
   reports, of the drownings in them hourly and the clutching
   skythrown hands billowing like sails eyewhite with madness?
   Or the low grinding of the women's bones as they crouch
   to feed the orders to the salesmen at the windows
   barking *Profit! Profit!* For

profit I would come into my office blind, issue orders blind,
   sell blind, renting hope to numbers whose flesh wrinkles
   to vinyl on the plastic of their bones. When Mary the
   half-wit secretary gave birth at my feet, her blue bastard
   snarled in her flowing hair, I simply ate the child
   disposing of the evidence and never noticed until now
   how her eyes have become tools of conception. Now when
   she trains on me those globeless sockets weeping amniotic
   shine I don't know what to say. I turn away

and see it's fall again. The trees outside are rich
   with validated policies, the streets are made of solid
   bonds, the buildings glow with immanence like structures
   blown to bits caught just as the first cracks appear:
   the windows fill with faces charged by the intent to speak,
   inhabited by hearts just wakened in their prisons
   and boneless to escape. The one

I had mistaken for the new clerk is half-Goat, his pimply brow
   broken by two horns, his human brains a pudding running
   through his hair. His eyes stutter like lightning as he
   clatters down the stairs after the receptionist who clatters
   naked just ahead of him, her split rump flashing vivid
   parts, blinking like a brakelight at rush hour. His horns

are carven gold, his breast the thin deep breast of Ram,
   his neck a hump of musky folds. Her flanks are trembling bright.
   From waist up she is Salmon now, gasping and shining.
   He takes her from behind, her mute jaws clack, eyes blank
   as coins. The stairwell floods with swirling darkness.
   Three *baaahs* and he snorts and drowns. She glides away,
   face locked in its silver grin. The office is chaos: banks
   of computers yawn and chatter, the operators buzz and glitter.

One more week of this and I am done. It's over just in time.
   I wouldn't care to say how much longer this profession of
   insurance is likely to remain valid, times being what they are.

I Go Out

*I believe we may safely assume that when
the rate of a man's inspiration drops
below a given level, he is dead.*

Dr. Christiaan Barnard

I go out looking for noses
   of various shapes and sensitivities,
   each to be kept in its own container,
   airless and labelled.

I go out for hands made and marred
   by their fortunes,
   broad working hands, the long
   thin hands of invalids and artists
   —these to be kept on cookie sheets.

I go out for eyes and knees,
   ears, navels, forearms and shins,
   genitals, clean-shaven cheeks,
   armpits and moustaches.

I go out night after night

returning by dawn, my car
filled with bags and jars,
plastic sacks and matchboxes,
identified donor by donor.

Until, Lord, I am ready at last
to make of these parts
one whole man.

A Dream of Snow
At the Zoo After a Visit to the Clinic

Trembling, as if with joy,
palsied in her shining chair,
the girl confronts the beasts that turn
and turn before each cage to stare.

Once long cages braced the legs
now brightly hidden in soft wools,
and from those early secret nights
when, innocent, she'd study how her
muscles dwindled till she slept,
she still remembers tingling tigers
creeping through her flesh in darkness,
stalking men of sticks and ice
in dreams of cold, dreams of snow.

Now the back-and-shoulder jungle parts
and brightens: A leopard's stare
blocks the bars. His urine-yellow eyes,
alert, sharpened by her helplessness,
stir her with their hopeless, deadly sympathy.

                              —Portland, Oregon—

Year of the Monkey: Night with a Veteran

1.
She sleeps and he imagines her asleep
in the next room
She sleeps and with her few words
dreams out loud among warm animals
false in the terror of darkness should she wake

She sleeps easily
now that her father who was gone
is home
He cannot sleep tonight

Restlessly he stares against his hands
hears wind in trees
the stealth of wind
tries to think it coaxes grass
from ground scorched by dry snow
here where there was snow

No snow where he has been

Fire and the stench of fire

2.
Late in a bright room
all the shades drawn, door locked
careful to keep his shadow
from betraying him against the shade
he listens
hears a car rip thin strips from the wet street
hears them tear up rags for bandages
sees the strange face bending down to his face
feels the breath
the blast
dim bodies near him smouldering
the reek of sulphur
bodies still as dolls

He feels the reaching hands
touch him as he disappears

Then the noise of newspapers wrapped around a wound
a thousand wounds
crowded
into darkness weeping without shame
more than he can comprehend
as he stares at his own healing hands

He wakes again to the nightmare
where a figure wrapped in paper
in the next bed stares
Again he watches
helpless
as characters he cannot understand
blur with a sudden strain
and the wide-eyed man is dead again

3.
Outside the branches barb with buds
The wind slips through
house after house unheard
moves from room to room
enters each sleeper, pauses
then starts across the lawns
between the houses of the neighbors sleeping
while in their dark garages
corrupting with rust of street-salt
cars hunch like unfinished tanks

While they sleep
and wind blows endlessly across their sleep
across a continent asleep
he listens

If he drew the shade, threw the window open
shouted
some of the sleepers nearest him would stir
and whimper

dream of someone crying
Fire! Fire!

But their sleep is undisturbed
his wife's sleep is unbroken
He knows what his hands mean
their groping in the darkness
their wooden stupor when he wakes
from dreams of bodies still as dolls
and he knows he'll endure it all

4.
It's late and he is tired
He shifts
to let his shadow lapse across the shade
and waits, trembling

Nothing
no sound but the wind
his own slow breathing
the strange face bending down to his face
and he sleeps
but dreams a dream of fire
he won't remember when he wakes
nor this crying out

The child hears him, stirs

The wound reopens

The stain spreads uncontrollably

Whiteout

In the dim glow of their igloo, still chanting
after months of the arctic night,
the fingers of three children dart and loop
in skillful string games. Their mother wipes
sweat from her glistening body
with skins and the precious shavings
from toys their father carved.
                                    A thousand yards away
in rising wind that flattens the fur back from his face,
he abandons his watch at the seal's breathing hole,
crouches and begins feeling
the long way home, guided by the iced contours of drifts
he reads with seal-skin hands, drawn on by faint songs
as the brilliance disintegrates before him.

Stoplight

Goggled yellow the cyclist's face
glares at a jaundiced world.
He cocks one leg and waits,
casual in his black girdle
of road-gear and skull helmet.

The mirrorbright exhaust
and handlebars reflect a grotesque
metaphor of caustic
likeness: *Buildings*
squat as cars like pike
dawdle first in still
water, then dart to strike
men minnowed in chrome.
Motion is his home.

Truck Talking Late

To His Partner

Hell no, it's not my
charming personality
—old Truck can be
¾ SOB
95% of the time,
stubborn as a mule
in a burning barn
the other half. I
can't ask no one
to listen. All
I can do
is talk and say
if you don't like it
stick it in your ear.
It's not my charm
has got me where I am.

And where am I?
            I'm nowhere,
a shorthair trucker
getting the shaft at work
from some longhair hippy.
Now I don't take no shit,
not off nobody. But I won't
stand up to you, buddy,
and argue—what the hell's
the use
to argue? Stone
on stone, that's what.

To His Wife

Now you just goddamn shutup.
You just shut up
and hear me out.
You got no evidence

not one shred
that I been carrying on
with other women. If
I been carrying on
you got no evidence, none.

To the Waitress

Me I do not know how to act.
Truck is one obnoxious SOB.
If you don't believe me
ask my daddy.

I don't think there's
anyone on this earth
more hot tempered,
more wild, more cold
to the core than me.

And no good goddamn woman
on this God's green earth
can straighten me out.
I can be good
three months, six months,
then some wildassed turn
comes on—I'm gone.
Just some wildassed turn,
I don't know.

To Himself

I wish to hell someone
had screwed my head on
different—I was born
bad blood
in a bad time getting worse.

I got the knowledge,
I got the will power,

I got the foresight.
If I want to step back
I can see it.
I get scared.
I get scared
of consequences. I take
the bit in my mouth
and it's like a sick dog
taking a belly of grass.

I never felt a day
in my life that
anybody really cared
if Truck stayed on the road
or went on over.

Voyeur

What is it they can
always find to say, the ones
who freeze the moment
I pull up to park
or those I happen on
in theaters, late, when
darkness is the third
member of the whispering
I never can quite hear,
overhear.
         How intimate
it seems because it is not
me to whom they speak
but to each other.
Or to themselves
in each other. When
the late late movie starts
to blind us with illusions,
when the stalled engine catches
and traffic resumes or the elevator
door opens and closes so

I hear no more,
then the empty light
around me changes—
not to red or green or
that maddeningly cautionary
amber, but to the exact
silverblackness of the mirrors
where I live, able to exist
only just as long
as I am looking on.

Kansasman
for Jean-Claude Marchant

1.
Me, I'm ATD.
                400 bucks
a month, I'm strictly cash.
I did my time for God
and Country, trashing Nam
—Now I trash the Man.

You understand?

2.
Just call me Kansasman.
This here is my old buddy "Red."
He has to slop these hogs
to get his bread. Now then,
just look at him.
All tidy in his uni
and all crazy in his head.
Gets off at night wired up
just like The Chair,
you know?
                Ready for action.

3.
I never punched a drunk

but once. Meaning who? Meaning
old Whizzer. Yeah, meaning the same.
Was I the lucky one that time!
He's a pro, know that? Or was.
Now I'd of gone down hooking,
bet your ass I'd go down
punching. Me, I wouldn't let
no man put me to bed snoozing.
If he had punched me, who knows?
I just might of gone crazy.
Staircrazy—walk right up the staircase
in that dude's chest! Remember
that Mercedes? Remember that!
Damn near tore my boot off
but I got both his headlights,
got the grill and radiator,
got the windshield
and....I got four teeth.
3 A.M. North Amsterdam.

Now that's a fact, my man.

4.
Cop come up once, says "Buddy,
empty out them pockets.
I wanna see you gotta gun."

I said, *Now listen, man.*
If I had a gun
you think I'd be through
shooting yet?

He says, "Where you from?"

Kansas.
"Where you headed?"

Kansas.
"And just where is this Kansas?"

Kansas
is the goddamn center of this country.

I told him that.

Rhetoric for the Dead

So you misjudged us
you who stood before
our monuments our faces
believing them
as we never dared believe

You offered
what you asked for
promised us challenged
did what you could do

And now we
have answered you
made in you
these new red mouths
Through them you utter
your final understandings
with us
chilling
catching fire

Now you know us
Now we have met
The charge has been made

We are astounded

Now that you are dead
we cannot do enough for you

For a Friend I've Lost Track Of

Today at work in a factory again
and hating it, I thought of you our senior year
who hated nothing, but lifted weights until your muscles
hunched your back and shoulders—even your hands:
stones—, muscles that froze you
into helplessness, afraid to fight for fear
        you'd kill someone,
afraid to love for fear of having to fight,
more and more alone through each year of high school,
gaining your crucial strength, your
        killing distance.

And I remember seeing you the last time 3 years
        out of school
in a park: *You run up to me, take my hand*
into the gentle granite of your hand
and lead me to see what you've done,
to admire the spinner hubcaps you've just waxed,
the car you've customized and no one but you has been in.
I look into the hubcap and see your metallic face
—Shining and shining and shining, there isn't
        a word it can say.

Swansong

"It feels good to be famous," he gasped,
face down in the dirt.
"I could've died of old age, gut-rot
or the preacher's threats...but
it's you that done me in.
Just think, Billy the Kid!
A notch in that big gun
sure beats a nitch
in the old lady's cupboard
—I love you for what you done."

And Billy grinned
and bid farewell
to another winner.

Matron to Poet

Mrs. X, who prides
herself on having
kept in touch
with things,

sits beneath a crown
of hair white as an
imbecile's conscience.
Encased in slick

black silk, wellfed,
childless midriff
shining
like a miner's sweaty cheek,

bright-eyed and concerned
that things go well
as such things can,
she smiles politely

at the poet, says,
"All things
considered, East Lansing is

industrious." And she can grin
diamonds.

Galveston Seawall Gang

Isn't this "Snake Island," the place
     a. where Lafitte used to hole up between raids
     b. where they aren't supposed to make buildings more than three
         floors high
     c. where the pirates stole the injuns' wives and the injuns ate
         the pirates
     d. where a hurricane and tidal wave made for overnight integration
         50 years before the Civil Rights Movement
     e. where we are now—and I don't see a snake or Indian or Pirate or
         any waves worth bothering with, just the machine gun
         chained to that grave and all these flowers

They come to the ocean
to be stopped
in time
by the wide grey lips
and the carelessly repetitious
smiling of the sea.

They, too,
foam at the mouth
like nude birds
dropped forever
through the air, flapping
their meaningless wings
like knives
against the fall.

Here at last is one other
who knows how it is
to have come so far, not
caring, not cared for,
knows how it is to arrive
like so many another
at the same place
in the same way
that no one notices.

They stand there,

beercans plugged
into their faces,
hair greased back
and hung carelessly down,
doing nothing,
missing nothing
from the corners of their eyes
where the sea slides in and in.

The Cave-In
for the one dead

1. *Foreman*

Yes, the walls *were* reinforced
that fell. Last night it rained, and the boys
were helping bail down to the firm ground
under mud as we stood at the edge,
hauling bucket after bucket
from the pit. I felt it, called,
jumped back as he looked up
and disappeared....
                        We couldn't dig,
no footing. It took us half an hour
to reach him. One man cried, I stared.
I'd stared if he were mine.
I never saw a body look so dead,
so much like clay, so much like what
he died in. I guess the planks
cracked overnight. But I'd have said
that hole was safe. In fact, I did.

2. *Man From The Emergency Rescue Squad*

Took ten minutes from the call,
fifteen more until we reached

his hand and pulled him free. Pulled
his body free. That's all there was,
and I knew that was all there'd
ever be.
                    Never seen a clay
cave-in before. I hope I seen
my last. His face was hard to tell
from what it laid in till I scooped
the mud from off his nose and mouth,
then his eyes. His eyes was shut,
thank mercy, but his mouth, it was
a scream jammed wide with mud.
How deep it got inside him's hard
to say, for sure. But he was dead.
Even so I tried to clean him out,
tried to clear his mouth and throat.
I had to try. Recessitator
cain't work till you do. Or then.
Machine ain't made to breathe life
into clay, but this one's worked some wonders
other times—I'll tell you that.

3. *Student*

It's such an inconvenience, all
this building. I told my parents, too.
But I was at my window watching
rain fall through the twigs
and buds and new green leaves—I thought
the coldsnap killed our vine till then—,
then it happened. I heard a shout,
a plopping sound, and saw the workmen
gather at the shallow crater
where a pit had been. But they
had made such noise since spring began—
that I ignored them, mostly. Once
a boy with blond hair laughed because
I tripped and nearly fell. I dropped
my books, and let him pick them up,
but only saw him digging once again.
I don't know who he was, but he

was nice....
                    At first I didn't know
a thing was wrong, imagine that!
Mostly, I ignore them.

4. *Other Man In The Pit*

Maam, I was with him when it happened.
I was with him, so I know—he couldn't
feel a thing. Believe me, I know
because they had to dig me free
and I was numb for half an hour,
or more. At least that much.
                    We'd just been makin
jokes, maam, makin jokes and laughin
like the Lord Hisself'd smile
to see us do. The men up top
were laughin with us, laughin, workin,
haulin buckets up to drop em
back.... But he was happy, maam,
he was strong and happy at the end.
It ought to count for something,
bein happy, young.... *Believe me,*
he didn't feel a thing. Not a thing.

5. *Same Man, Late In The Winter*

There's times I think it's every night
since spring I had that dream—them
pullin that boy out, and leavin me.
I don't know why a man dreams
such a thing night after night. When
I told my wife, before she left me,
at first she'd listen, let me talk
and tell her how it felt. The weight
of all that clay, the tons and tons
soft as mud but heavy, baby,
so heavy, risin higher, higher, full

of stones that squeeze my back and legs
until they snap like sticks that drive
clean through my skin. And tryin
to breathe and breathin all that muck
into your face, holdin back but breathin,
breathin deeper. Deeper.... Then
she'd turn away and say to sleep.

Can you imagine sleep with dreams
like that? I'd lie awake, I'd lie
awake all night and hear her breathin,
afraid to shut my eyes and hear
the buckets fall again, or see
them pull the body from the mud
and clean the face. To shut my eyes
and watch, and recognize myself.
But please, don't turn away, don't turn away.

Arc Welder Out in the Country

The darkness at midnight
—moonless, 20 below—

is that black ice of
interstellar space

through which breath
falls in crystals

when my widowed neighbor
sets to work. He

crouches to battle havoc
in a crackle of flashes

that hollow out bright caves

of visibility

the eye cannot maintain
constant

against the stutter
of that star

so hot steel melts
like wax

which briefly glows
at the core

of each failed effort
to create

out of the Pennsylvania dark
a universe

the eye open at midnight
can close to

twice.

Pox: A Prognosis

It starts with a spot on your cheek
that festers and scabs

over. It draws the good skin
tight, then

pulls it in. It looks
like a navel

sunk in your cheek. Soon
with its feeding it pulls

your face awry. The nearest eye
shifts toward it.

This will distort your
ordinary sense of things

until one night as you sleep,
dreaming of being whole,

the spot consumes
the troublesome eye and when you awake

you see clearly
what's left of the world to see.

Next the nose, the other eye,
the corner of your lips.

This is the worst time of all:
Blind you breathe through the edge

of your mouth
and whistle as you breathe, listening

with the ear that's left
to the pitch of the whistle rise.

Your whole face
is consumed and where your face

once was,
scalp stretches to cover.

Of course you do not see.
You do not breathe or hear.

But as long as you pretend
you can,

no one will seem to care
or scream when you appear.

"To Whom Shall I Speak and Give Warning?"

These are the women walking and walking
hopelessly the promised streets.
Gazing back at shopwindows and bloody meats
cellophaned at their fingertips,
hoarding all their stamps, receipts,
and memories of weekend trips,
these are the women walking.

These are the men, their husbands, working,
crediting their daily lives
and nightly dying. Into the sad calm of their wives
they press the automatic seed, investing
in the sheltered womb that craves
her startling daughter-Queen, his son-King.
These are the men and women, getting and spending.

Who are the children born
and bearing
all the generations of desire?

2. How the Pygmy Forest Works

"and that's how we got out"

"And They Swam and They Swam"
for Bruce McGrew

Well the first thing they noticed was how those minnows
   in the biggest schools got sluggish and how
   it's the sluggish ones the pickeral pick off first.

"Interesting," they said.

Well they took an ordinary minnow, destroyed half
   its brain, stuck it back in the water: It swam,
   eccentrically, but it swam—nobody picked it off,
   it moved too much. Unpredictably.

"Interesting," they said.

Well it jerked along and came to a large school
   of minnows, sluggish ones picked off left and right
   by pike and pickeral. He jerked on by, they
   spotted him and did what he did, jerked
   and pulled off the most outrageous flips.

"Hmmm," they said. "No minds of their own. Interesting..."

Well the school flitted and darted free of the big fish,
   flashing wonderfully in and out of sight: Lost
   their predators, lost the scientific observers.

"Interesting," they said. "They're altogether
   out of sight—Even the pike can't find them!
   But where'd they go?"

Interested?

The Lord's Circus
As told by the waitress at an all-night diner in west Texas

One night last year, about this time,
nothing but that busted hunk
    of neon moon out there
and nothing in here but these roaches
    in the cups and me,
there was this pack of bikers come
    roaring in off the road in their
    black leather all
hungry for a good time and figuring
    I was it.
One wore most his own teeth
strung out like a Cheshire grin
across his bare chest and drooled
    in a fancy lace hankie
when he laughed. Beer and fries
was what they ordered but I knew
    it was trouble coming up
when Hank pulled in, them trailer
    lights on his big rig
blinking like the Lord's circus,
the rumble of that warmed-up diesel
    muttering
like lions in the dark.

Now Hank's no fool. He seen the hidden
    knives glitter
in their eyes, the steel-toe boots
    dangling from the stools
they spun around on, staring.
He just set down grinning back and
    when the drooler
took it in his head to stir up
    salt in Hank's black coffee
he still grinned and there they set,
    bumper to bumper,
while that engine muttered

like a pride of lions
in the dark outside.

And when they run him down
name by rude name, insult by insult,
he just grinned, his knuckles
    whiter than that cup
dwarfed in his hands.
They had their fun and skinned
    him out with words
and when they let him go
they howled so loud that not one
    noticed how
he backed that flashing rig of his out,
toppling the whole row of bright
    chained bikes
like chrome dominoes and crushing
    every one
before he drove off in the dark again,
lighting up the highway with his grin.

One Sunday
A grandfather's tale

One Sunday, when the quick rain fell,
what happened by a scarcely dampened dusty road
on grass still dry under an oak
is that they heard the restless bay mare
snort and stamp, jangling her harness
where their buggy stood in silence, halfway home,
and I was born in earshot of the next spring's Sunday bells.

Why That Black Girl Picking Delta Cotton
Will Be a Nurse

Aint got no nurses in Bolivar County.
Aint got no doctors
aint got nothing.
You got all these babies dying
on account that Miss Corrine
dont know what she about.
Thats how my Ma died
with my baby sister.
               That morning
when the moon still shine
my Pa woke me up
told me go fetch Miss Corrine.
I aint knowed nothing about no babies
I warnt no more than eight
but all the other womens they come
they aint knowed more than me.
My Ma screaming and screaming
and them saying oh god oh my god
praying like they aint
rightly know what they about.
Old Aunt Effie come out once
say she aint never seen nothing
like the pain Ma had to take.
When Pa took off for Mound Bayou
he done clean out of his head.
He took Mr. Jeffrey's truck
something Pa aint never did.
When Pa run out I run in
to look quick. Lord it was blood
ever which-a-way and Ma just staring
her eyes bout to pop.
She had done stop yelling.
She look at me and aint even knowed me.

Hear tell that doctor aint want to come none.
Hear tell my Pa done pick him up and brung him.
I reckon he'd a put Pa in the lockup

cept when he seen Ma
it cleaned all the evil outta him.
He say the baby was in wrong.
He say Ma shoulda been cut in her belly
but who knowed it? Miss Corrine aint.
Aint never admit she aint knowed either.
She still killing people and they baby.
How she gone know?

Warnt much to Pa after that.
He just begun to stare
like something in him wrong too.
He aint never forget how he aint know
to do nothing. Folks say
he die same day as Ma
just had to wait longer to get buried.

Aint got no family. Only me.
By the time I get outta school
I gone have enough to get outta here.
I reckon I can get work
in Jackson or Memphis, one.
That'll pay my way.
Aint no big city can keep me.
I gone be nursing right here
in Mound Bayou if I lives.

Bipolar Hermaphrodite's Ritual for Walking Past Nine Windows in the Asylum's East Wing

1

Walking my face electric and brave
with alcools of turquoise and opal

walking my legs magic and bright
as chrome-handled umbrellas

walking my feet and knees
walking my shell-white belly

2

walking my talent for walking
through rainlight

through sealight through hairlight
and treelight

walking my talent for walking
I think every step of the way

3

What am I wasting these
fine steps on earth for?

Why am I giving such breath
to the air? Why

am I treating these myriad eyes
blank as unminted coins

4

to me? These doctors
with pedestrian tastes

love their dogs
clipped and curled

like their women.
Lord, their women!—

5

they love L'eggs
and attend Sexy Rexy

religiously on Saturday night
then flirt Sunday morning

with the holy Ghost,

gobbling down the Host

6

like a piece of breakfast toast
—a sop for Bloody Mary

which is the hair of the dog.
They jog in pairs, in place.

They are the plastic-faced
stiff darlings of the mannikin race.

7

My face is powdered blue
as the dazzle of sky

where my eyes are opals
like twin suns shining

through the unpredictable weather
of my manic laughter

8

as I walk my talent for walking
and parade the blade of my outrage

slicing my way through the crowds
who open like pages of cheese

and point like the hands
of a compass

9

crying out like lemmings
who catch their first whiff of the sea

as they follow me
as they follow me

walking my talent for walking
away, away, away.

A Step in the Dance

Wind moves blindly
through the casual hair
of the hobo immobile
on the moving train
—this man
who does not move,
who gets where he's going.

Accident on the Highway at Night

His mind smears with stars.
Numb, his body is the earth
spilling on itself. Then
eyes: moving mouths: faces flashing
blood. Swaying, the far clear moon.

Making Way

I was edgy, pulling out of a parking lot
into Tucson rush hour traffic in Frog,
my old green Cougar with its skyroof wide,
my faithful 90 pound Oscar's head beside mine,
when I noticed the teenager noticing us
and nudging his buddies in the red pickup,
all of them craning around to see
the bearded guy and his dog, and just then
Oscar sneezed his magnificent flailing firehose
sneeze that covers a 180 degree arc nicely,
my face at about 160.
                   Off flew my glasses, and as I wiped
his high velocity slobber
from cheek and forehead, those kids— maybe Apache,
maybe Pima or Tohono O'odham, all smiling like
brown Buddhas— left room for me to pull in.

How could I ever forget the joy in their smiles
at seeing this anglo-honkie get it from his dog
like that, how their broad gentle faces widened
with amusement, how their dark eyes glowed?
And how I couldn't even begin to feel outrage
at unmannered Oscar, whose cousin after all
is old man Coyote— rule-breaker without equal,
who, even in rush hour traffic, is alive and well,
whose tail is still wagging at the end of the 20th Century?

Passing Go

Bowlegged behind her cane
on Market street
in late afternoon
she waits as sure
of a streetcar
as cactus is of rain,
patchwork satchel
vivid against the dark
wedge of her coat.

Mist curls at
her swollen ankles
like a lap dog
she ignores.

As the racket pauses
she hauls herself aboard,
lurches
when it starts.

*Hey lady
you didn't pay!*

She halts, spins round,
points the cane. *You men,
you're all alike—
All you want to do is fuck!*

She slips into a seat,
winks at the lady
stiffened beside her.

Whispers in her ear,
*Works every time now
don't it, dear?*

Cliff Diver

Consider the diver,
his careful fall
through fear
toward the thrill
of water glittering
among rocks. Death
is for the hesitant
who stumble.
            The one
most alive
graces that fall
with consciousness
and skill. He
wings his fears,
learns from them
on the long way down
—hawkheart soaring
in the earthbound body of man!

Suomo Wrestler

Barrelled in muscle,
cat-eyed, huge,
charged with the calm
central to a storm,
he lives a ritual feast
of gorgeous energies.

All that he has he shares
with the silent presence
who validates each meal
in the void of famine,
generates with each muscle
the vision of his own
fly-brightened bones,
appointing his smile
with the signifying edge
of a pride quick to kill
gestures of vanity.

Aware of his body
like a garden hung
on racks of bone,
whose veins are vines
that redden through
the beating lungs
and brain that blossom
from the spine, aware
of the closed
circuitry of blood,
the warrior feasts
on knowing, knows and lives.
His lungs inspire
and translate into power
each fatal breath of air.

At war with time
his will wins, hour by hour,
until the years win

from his body
such an instant grace
that eyes able to see
him move see through
the trance of time,
as through a dream,
one man awake.

For the World's Strongest Man

> Vasili Alexeev, Olympic Champion weight-lifter,
> lives in a rural mining region of the U.S.S.R.
> where he trains, enjoys reading Jack London, and
> pursues his interest in hydroponic gardening. He
> has developed hybrids of the rose and tomato which
> are named after him.

1.
A mist fine as the hair of infants
rises from the grasses,
surrounds your town like a dream
round the head of a great sleeper.

But you, Vasili Alexeev, you do not sleep yet,
you who are a family man, private as a bear,
whose deep breast gives deep laughter
among your neighbors, the shopkeepers and miners.
How tenderly your hands, ominous as cave-ins,
tucked in your children and your wife tonight.

You do not sleep. You see beyond your window
a scar of cloud tucked under the moon's eye.

Your hydroponic heart is afloat in your life's blood.

2.
What a man would grow must flourish first in his heart.

Beside your home, whose lights one by one go out,
glows another house, translucent and frail,
whose constant light burns through the coldest Russian dark.
Here you house members of your family
        from that other kingom,
the roses and tomatoes bearing your name,
both red as the blood feeding the broad leaves of your muscle.

The rose opens from its center outward, as a hand
        opens to expose an offering;
but the other, should it open, spoils its gift, and so
        turns inward like a fist,
swells into the edible muscle of tomato.

If one nourishes love
the other feeds the lovers,
their eventual sons and daughters.

So here are the rose of the eye and the rose of the belly,
the rose of persons and the People's rose.

In the waters of your floating gardens both prosper and grow.

3.
There is the deep night of the earth
        into which your townsmen pass
                in shifts, passing the grazing

cattle that stand among the slag heaps
        underneath the claw of the moon
                where grasses silver in the mist,

and there is the deep night
        neither time nor place describes,
                when you put aside your book

of tales (*To Build A Fire?*
        Sea Wolf?) and, isolate
                as a stone floating in darkness,

you sit awhile, perfectly still,
     hearing the house's soft breathing,
          before you gird your belly, bind your wrists.

"Enough to Make a Running Shark to Sigh"

Next come fairmaids
Bra thusty jaades
As maade our oozles dry
An ling an haake
Enough to make
A raunin' shark to sigh
               from "The Ballad Of Tom Bawcock's Eve"

In Mousehole, on Tom Bawcock's Eve,
tourists come from miles to drink

in both local pubs, loudly singing
the wrong songs. A stranger

in search of friendly strangers,
I walk from the one crowded bar

to the other, then wander the harbour,
its half circle the oldest in Cornwall.

Drinkers everywhere tonight
are tight as the seven

sorts of fish
crammed into Tom's Starry Gazy Pie.

I'm startled by one fisherman
stout as a mast, dark as a post,

who will not sit
in his haunts tonight. He steps

back into the alley, black eyes fast
on the booming seawall

where storm waves rear
like pale familiars

vast as monsters, luminous
in the Christmas lights.

They crash against handfitted stones
the tourists in leather coats shun.

The fisherman stands in attendance,
cold, sober, and patient.

—Mousehole, Cornwall—

Fisherman

A woman comes
to watch her lover pull nets from the sea.

His back bulges with ocean waves
contenting her a moment while his body,
black against the sun,
is swollen with such power
the slow dull sea around him trembles light.

She drops to her knees
and waits with sea-light blowing in her hair
and with her skirt
she shades what she has brought.

Noon.

He sees her, shrugs the stone-gleam of his shoulder
and drags the living weight up onto land,

each wave trying to drag it back.

He joins her in dry grass beyond the sand.

Wine from a bottle tall and cool
in its wrapping of wet rags, a loaf,
a wedge of cheese, an apple and a knife.

While sunlight plays on fish dying
in thrashing brilliance
he chews and sees her eyes darken for him
and he is glad and laughs.

They are young
and neither seems to notice
the distant net
flashing,

the frantic sound of a thousand fingers snapping.

A pale gull slowly wheels a relic circle
then is gone.

A Shy Phenomenologist Breaks the Ice

Where there was nothing
but your silence waiting

now there is a green skull
jeweled by green eyes

breaking the reflection
of cloud on a pond.

A fly darts down, disappears,

the face submerges.

Cloudlight heals the water
with its stillness

as our faces reappear
upon that surface, gazing

deeply into themselves
in search of the argueable frog.

And things are as they should be.
The cheek-to-cheek. The mystery.

How the Pygmy Forest Works
Fragment of a Conversation Overheard

We were lost there
in the pygmy forest
calling for help
and nobody heard us.
Finally the only way out
was on our hands and knees
the stuff was growing so thick
and that's how we got out
was on our hands and knees.

The End of Winter in an Old Neighborhood

for Sena

1.
Today is not quite spring
but now the Marchlit windows
widen,
       show the screen
of thin dry twigs that flinch
as sparrows hop.

     Cracking buds
perch
like beetles split
        for flight:
           Gables jut,
                 bay windows
               belly out against the wind.

2.
Today from Minnesota came a letter
from grandmother:

     Bright storms raged around us
but they missed us and we have
               a lovely Sunday morning
nice and cool
         though saddened by the stroke a patient had
Last night she lost her voice and cannot move
her eyes
       My boy you'd see my second childhood
if you could see me now   *I crawl along in bed*
quite on my own
          and in my infant fashion am quite free
    I feel
so free
     after these months stiffened in
traction and ridiculous in casts

We even have some fun
  The wind changes direction
often so the nurses run   opening and closing windows
asking how we feel   too warm   too cool   Too late
to write much more now
I must nap

  And now we've had our evening meal
One hears the cart that clatters like so many bones
and pauses
    and the opening and closing
of the doors to all the rooms as it passes   stops in silence
starts moving room by room along the hall
                At the end
        it waits for us
to finish
    then the clatter once again
of glass on hard white steel

    They say my bones are hardening again
Like sponge they were   So soft I couldn't stand
                  They wouldn't
hold my body up   I weigh just ninety-five now like I did when
I was twenty and all day long
            I wear a nightie   this one or
another but they're laundered here so often that they fade
bleached without light
            And how I miss the color
        of my hair
      "Scarlet mane" your mother called it
    and your father "Burning bush"
So short now   They keep it
cut so short

      It's good to be in bed
with the moonlight on the snow
                Two pillows prop my head
and the snow is like a sheet that wraps the world   The room
is rather dim   The other patients sleep
                and I must close

or I will wake and think this letter was a dream
and write again and say this all again
but I can feel our winter's
nearly over

3.
A green vine flares along the twigs
steady on its amber claws

and as the branches heave
the hooktips catch:
it rides.
The seasons
tremble everywhere.

Life Sentences

Existentialist

I'm the absurd chameleon, trying
to match the colors of the fire
instead of leaping out.

Stoic

The madder I get the calmer I become
until I am a stone
no on can throw.

Nun Viewing A Rainbow

Now is the perfect time
for the laying aside of old
habits of black and white.

Apocalyptic Pessimist

Trees of the earth uproot themselves,

crying out dead fruit
      and the bones of birds.

Narcissist

What's a nice guy
like me doing
      in a face like this?

Politician

There's more to these things,
you know, than
      meets the press.

Master Teacher

Imagine
trying to explain air
      to a lung.

Jester

Who knows
what evil larks
      in the hurts of men?

Cynic

I chew more
than I swallow
      with my bite.

Old Prospector

All gold is fool's gold
—*If you're so smart
      how come you're rich?*

Epicurean Idealist

I am all appetite, a net

flung to catch fish
        that catches stars!

Mystic

Rain speaks to the grass.
I overhear it
        and my ears get wet.

Author
        after Fellini

The oyster's view of the pearl?
—It crowds him
        in his shell.

Sometimes Heaven is a Mean Machine
for Wayne Sloan

It is like riding Death and not dying

It shudders, snarls and roars like an iron lion,
it shines like the chromed bones of a bull.

At night its single headlight
rakes across the highway like the lowered horn
        of a charging unicorn.

It looks like Death waiting for a taker.

You take it, you ride.

All day, all night for years
while the bright arcs of your breath flex
        into curves repeating earthshapes,
        you ride, the road informing you.

You ride
your own death and you do not die.

It shines and you ride its shining.

Song of the Woman and the Butterflyman
for Shoshanna

Here the woman
walked over the earth
among the nights and days
beautiful clothes upon her skin
beautiful skin upon her bones
        and from the center of her bones
        had the child sprung
                whom she carried with her
                        over the earth

Here the woman
walked over the earth
and the grasses bloomed
underfoot behind her
and rivers ran shining
        with quick light
        wakened by her grace
                and the child was happy
                        where she walked

Here the woman
walked over the earth
and entering a valley
she saw the butterfly
rising and falling
        in flowering grasses
        and skimming the river
                its beauty disturbing her
                        where she walked

Here the woman
walking the valley
followed the butterfly
followed faster   lay
the child down in shade
        to follow the butterfly
        over the long green grasses

across the river
where she ran

Here the woman
following and running
now swift as a doe
removed her clothings
one by one   moving away
as they fell sinking
into the shaken grasses
clouds of pollen golden
where she ran

Here the woman
running through the valley
found the butterfly
waiting   found it vivid
and it was a warrior now
who found the dark center
of her bones empty
and filled it with his shining
where she lay

Where she lay
she rose still in his arms
as he turned saying *Hold*
here as we go—his hand
showing hers the place—
or your spirit will be lost
Now the woman was happy
and did as she pleased
while they flew

While they flew
she held as he had shown
and she was not ashamed
naked to the eyes of the sky
and the sun looked and saw
and moon and stars looked and saw
and a day passed

and a night passed
and she held

Woman of earth held
and she was not ashamed
to be available to the grasses
and entries of the water
and approaches of the air
then she saw all around her
everywhere   everywhere
the wheel of the butterflies
and she fell

And she fell
through a valley of the sky
whose floor was the flow
endlessly of butterflies
turning and returning
opening her eyes to the shining
that opens forever
around her   and opens her
and opens   opens

VIII. C O O T

for old Ben Fuljamin and coots everywhere

"Great things are done when men and mountains meet;
This is not done by jostling in the street."

William Blake

Meeting Coot

Nope, not hardly local.
                           Buggywhip
in a world of powerbrakes,
that's me. Unplucked old coot
in a world of sitting ducks
and pumped-up turkeys. Me,
I'm crazy. Crazy like that loon
who spends the livelong night
trying to decide which moon
to court—the far one in the air
or the nearer one in water—
so it clammers back and forth
and back and forth it yodels
while the brightmouthed fox
stands baffled on the shore.

Nope, not these parts.

Coot's Uses for His Shirts

My clothes come from my needle,
some, and some from the Good Will.
I'd rather have a shirt
after it's had the smell
of factory washed out, some life
worn in.
                My own manufacture—
as you see, it ain't fancy.
Trousers loose enough
to squat down in without no rip
to scare the creatures off
I squat to visit with.
And look: This shirt's so cheap
no man'd need to think twice
to tear it for a tourniquet

or wipe off his face on it.
Why this here shirt of mine's so full
a man could hoist it for a sail
if he had a wind with him.
If he had a mind to, I should say.
There's always wind
to find a man who's stranded,
and knows it, and knows what
other uses things are for.

How Coot Got His Start, He Says

I was a young man once—
set out for gold
like steelhead head to sea
or fleas make for a sleeping dog.
Worked two years in dry goods,
staked myself to a mule
and all the vittles we could tote.

Didn't have no map neither,
except the one the Lord made
and set out there
for any fool like me
to light out into.
And I lit.

How Words Taste and What Food Means

You listen to most people talk.
You try to taste their words:
Storebought. All dried out,
or froze up like them foods
plastered with lists of poisons.
Anything that ain't natural
is poison. Ask a coyote. Tasteless
stuff a packrat wouldn't touch,
cramful of all them cancers
of the spirit and the flesh.
And then you start to rot,
and what?—They try to sell
you paint to make what smells
so bad look right.

Coot Tells It Like It Never Was

A desert in late August
must be a holy place.
Before the first sunset
I seen a miracle:
The eggs I brought
was all hardboiled
in mule sweat.
                    By fall
we was holed up
in the Bloody Christ Mountains.
By Christmas I was eating bear
and looking at the mule
with a new eye. Until
she disappeared one night.
Ate her anyhow, turns out,
by eating me a grizzly
had four shod hooves
still kicking in his gut!

Coot's Lonelieness Coot's Gold

Come spring and I hit
on various things—loneliness
and gold among them. Gold
enough to keep fire
burning in me. Loneliness
enough to dull the shine.
I dreamed like anyone how one day
I'd come into a town
with ore as rich and bright
as in my dreams, rich enough
to strike the townsfolk dumb
and shut up those loud looks
I had to pass through
when I came to town.

Well, there was one
who looked on me so different
that I married her. Or
tried to.
            Like trying
to lassoe a cloud it was—
both of us being clouds,
no rope in sight. So,
past the first three kids
it couldn't last. Some
new wind blew.
She stayed her way,
I went mine.

"Like Going Home"

And this time getting
back amongst the mountains
was like going home.
Sitting by a stream
watching my line
was how I shopped.
Listening to coyotes
was my radio.
         I could read
the weather by the moon
and learn more
from a scraped stone
or bird chatter
than all that gossip
neighbors like to dote on.

My cabin was no castle,
but just mine.
And it was mine
because my hands knew
every stump
on every slope I drug
them logs down off of.
Not because of paper.
I didn't have no paper.
What I had was distance
on all that, for a time.

Coot Takes a Look at *COSMOPOLITAN*

Look here now, at this magazine:

> *A Blush So Real No One Will Know*
> *It's Not Your Own...*

Me, if I was to see a lady
stand there glowing
like the moon all night,
I'd suspect consumption first off.
And bad conscience, second.

Or this:

> *What To Tell Your Husband*
> *If You Put On Weight—*
> *While Having An Affair*

Whatever it is they tell her
she should say, she'd need
to learn to pronounce it in shotgun
if she was mine, cause
that's what she'd be talking
into the ears of.

How Coot Came to Speak Bear

How many winters
come and gone up there
you'd have to read yourself
from off my walls,
if they still stand.
I lost interest in counts
after awhile.
                    What I did
those years up there,
mostly I've forgot. I wonder
if there's ever rivers learn
to know their banks and beds?
But I do know I looked out
over valleys like a hawk looks
—eyes on fire, heart at peace,
the belly in me lean as a pinecone.

What else I did
was look a lot in water,
watch how fire is,
learn something about wind
from how I saw a bear sniff
out my coming one day
on a cliff. Two greased friends
at high noon in late August
couldn't have passed
there on the ledge
where me and that bear
did pass, neither of us
willing to retreat.
We spoke first is how
we knew we could.

To know what we had said,
you'd have to been
there, too. And spoken bear.

Coot and the Quiet

Most of my adventures
was of the quiet sort.
Like noticing one night
how my old cedar dipper
was as full of stars
as water. Then I drank.

A man inside four walls
all his natural life
cannot drink stars.
Even the full moon
can't touch his sleep
with dreams the likes
of which only a creature
knows, a creature touched
with what it is
that lights up a man's skull
like fire lights up a cave.

Coot and the Golden Arches

Fast food, fast cars, fast money
—it's all fast talk.
                    Now,
take ideas. They're just like grub.
Until they reach your blood
they ain't digested proper. The gent
who'd never be caught dead talking
with Egg McMuffin in his mouth,
he'll talk a snow goose south in June
with notions he's still chewing on.

It takes a touch of patience
before the cut-throat trout rocks
back on his haunches
roaring like a bear with fishy breath.
But time will tell.

"Don't Matter to a Dog He Won't Reach China"

Can't teach old dogs fancy
new tricks. Can't teach
an old dog tricks at all.
He just ain't interested
in tricks.
        He'd rather
chew on bones or follow
real scents down
real holes and start to dig.
Don't matter to a dog
he won't reach China. China
ain't what he's after,
after all. He's only wanting
something cool to do
while the sun shines. And digging
down on in is cool enough.

Coot and the Sperm Bank

This whole notion of banks is sad,
sorry as a sinner Sunday morning.
I'd never trust no man who scrubs
his nails with anything I grub for.
And this business of "donors," now
don't it make the whole affair smack
of righteous charity, alms for the poor?
Money's bad enough, but now they're
setting up a whole new generation
to be strangers.
        It's sad all right.
Sadder than the phoney fires
they burn up iron logs with
in bars where youngsters sit
all night working up a sweat
to record music. Hot enough,

that fire, to brand a bawling calf,
but it will leave your cockles cold
and it don't fill up air
with the right scent. A good fire,
you can read it like a book,
your eyes and ears, nose and skin,
all working at the same time.
There's a deal of history in fire
and hints about the future.
                              Lord,
I'd dread to look into the eyes
of any son of mine
my Missus had withdrawn
from some Nobel genius stranger
who couldn't even leave his name.
You got to tend a fire once you set it
or it will run amok seeking you out.

How How Uncle Lucky Got That Way
for Ralph E. Spurlock

How'd he get that name, you say?
I'll tell you how.
                    Our people
back in Michigan got word
how there was good to be had
over there in Jordan, Montana,
so they packed up
their women and the wagons
and set out at first thaw.

What should of took weeks
took months. Gumbo, you see.
Had to scrape the gumbo off
their wagon wheels ever few feet
or horses couldn't haul em.
Arrived early June, they did,
the blue-joint hay hand-high,

and started harvesting
soon as they had shelter.
Took a mite of a while—
didn't have no pitchforks
nor the means
to put it up.
Come fall, though,
they sent uncle on to Miles City
with the works, to trade out
for winter supplies and maybe
a barrel of whiskey spirits
to keep their own from lagging.

Well, he was gone some time,
he was, and come back
a hoopin and a hollerin
with four whisky barrels
in the wagon. Nothin more.
Them barrels wasn't sea-cured
so all the way they rolled round
and broke up and run dry.

Winter comin on, them hills afire
with warnin—pretty to look at,
right painful to consider.
My daddy and the others,
they like to killed him
then and there—
lucky they needed
ever sorry pair of hands
they could find those days.

Lucky fellah, they'd say later
when his name come up.
Lucky none
a them horses died
he'd taken off to Miles City.
Brought em back
lookin like they'd gone
the full five thousand,
grazing as they had to

on what it is a horse
can graze on tied
to the hitchin rail
of the Miles City saloon.
But they was alive still,
if worse the wear,
and he was some worse too,
so they didn't shoot him.

And lucky they got buffalo
enough to stretch out
through the lean months
or they'd et his ass
for Easter, sure. Lucky
for him, is what they said
all that winter. And the Lucky stuck.

Coot and the Big Time

Well, it was skiing
finally brought me down
and who'd of thought?
Folks bought a neighbor
mountain and brought
all those strangers in
to make it right
for still more strangers,
and they came. Just a few
at first, like the first flakes
of a big one. Then a town,
the river dammed up,
rammed down its own throat
to flood the valley
with lit ski slopes, stores,
stores, stores. A city,

mind, a whole blessed city
just for people passing through.

By and by they asked,
of course, for papers.
By and by
I told them
what they knew.
Not one of them
had lived a winter
drinking boiled snow.
Not one knew what
the thirst is
a star quenches.
Not one spoke bear.
Nor hardly English neither,
to judge by what them
and their piles of paper
had to say
of what was legal nowadays
and just. Them,
they just spoke Book.

Coot's Re-entry

My wife had long since
taken leave of nonsense,
died.
      Our children,
well, they said *Come on*,
and by their lights
they meant it, too.
But, it wasn't long
before it seemed
they were not mine,

I was not theirs.

I'm not quite sure
just where I'll go
next yet. But go I will.
I feel a shrinking in my bones
that would mean snow,
if this was a place
with seasons.
                    Pasadena?
Listen, friend. Pasadena
ain't seen snow
since Jesus drove the bus.

Coot's Lode

It's a funny thing, you know?
Prospecting a lifetime long
and finding out about
the kind of gold there is
still in the wilderness
that no one can haul out
by mule or truck or train
or spend anywhere it is
that men are spending,
to have the knowledge
of that lode by heart
and know no human tongue
to reveal it in.
                    Lord,
I've come too far by now
to trust in maps for others
and grown too worn, or nearly so,
to make it by myself.

Who could I tell?

IX.   W E S T

"that coming world"

SEATTLE (Seathl), Dwamish chief, spoke to Isaac Stevens, Governor of Washington Territory, 1854.

Day and night cannot dwell together. A few more moons; a few more winters—and not one of the descendants of the mighty hosts that once moved over this broad land or lived in happy homes, protected by the Great Spirit, will remain to mourn over the graves of a people once more powerful and hopeful than yours. . . . And when the last Red Man shall have perished, and the memory of my tribe shall have become a myth among the White Man, these shores will swarm with the invisible dead of my tribe, and when your children's children think themselves alone in the field, the store, the shop, upon the highway, or in the silence of the pathless woods, they will not be alone. At night when the streets of your cities and villages are silent and you think them deserted, they will throng with the returning hosts that once filled and still love this beautiful land. The White Man will never be alone.

1.   Along The Coast

"We call them stones so we will not remember."

Dear Jeffers
A Note from Sheridan to Carmel-By-The-Sea

It's a long way from the queer remote silence-making *quawk*
of that heron your words snagged on the wing
as I was being born, Jeffers, decades ago,
in a Minnesota blizzard, and you were in a squall of rage
near Big Sur in the place no longer your place—
      as you forsaw, dragging stone after stone
to your tower nonetheless
from the live surf and froth of your own sweat.

Edged in now
by homes No-Man built to live in—high priced suckertraps
for those successful in that coming world you shunned and decried
poem after bitter poem—your stone tower, Jeffers,
      even your stone tower
raised by hand toward the high blue home
of those beloved hawks
toward whom you turned and turned your falcon of a face
      for evidence of worthiness,
is gone into their hands, their pockets,
enhanced by your famous hatred, the prices rising
with your skydriven fistlike poems exactly abhorring them.

Where I am, in Wyoming still magnificent with wilderness
no sea has breathed on for millions of years,
      the old forces
finding a new grip soon will ream out
ranchers and farmers bewildered by profits sudden as true
      strokes, making way for holes
into which men hungry for the good life
      will descend, innocent
of your hawks, gulls, godlike stallions, and women
with wild eyes, kind eyes, will tend them
as some die, most prosper
      in the ways men do these days, surrounded
by the crown jewels of the age—
      appliances and gadgets designed to make
life careless. And they work, dear Jeffers. They do work.

The City of Dreaming of Horses

Each dawn we watch the bus descend
through lifting mist, come shining down
an emerging hill's decline to the sea.
We mount its trembling steps, feed
the chattering meter quarters, sit,
begin to sleep—but first sway round
our brightly curved tidal bay,
begin the lifting road up through
the hillside pastures, passing every
day the dewdrenched buckskin mare
who comes to lean against the leaning
fence and stare as, from our serial
windows, we stare back before we
enter the city dreaming of horses.

On the Tidal Ledge

Near a headland
while I closed my eyes and listened,
I heard them cry, drowning in the wind.
I looked, and the illusion disappeared.
They hovered bright above the waves
where cresting edges shattered
on gusts of wind sky alone imagined
while I watched.

Excited, but cold,
I hunched a bit and moved on toward a cove
where the tidal ledge is pocked
with cup- and basin-sized pools.
I found a ringed anemone
open in a vulgar bulge of moss on a rock.

Curious with an idle kind of jealousy,
malicious,

I teased the ancient total mouth
with little stones.
Wiser than I'd known
the anemone ignored the bait of pebbles,
then closed around my finger
sinking shut against its stone. I felt it
fix its tiny hooks.
My finger stung, I jerked it free.
The flesh had barely tingled,
but I was tight with dread
at how cold seaflesh is
and how it feels: It clings like a kiss.

I watched the soft jawbelly
dilating slowly
on its deep bald face of stone,
the cilia, like eyelashes, wavering
with hunger on their round blind lid.
Swollen wide, it spilled out grains of sand
that tumbled toward a growing pile
already at the bottom of the pool.

I moved beyond decaying stone
and trapped water, its creature.
                              I left it
waiting at the temperature of death, and tried
to find again wings and eyes shining
in a knowledge of the light.

Retreat Near Mt. Tamalpais, California

> Searchers were unable to locate the driver's body
> although at one point it was believed blood had
> been discovered leading from the wreckage at the
> bottom of the cliff into woods toward a distant
> monastery.

There is a place, a valley
dropping through hills
toward the sea,

where a man—whose body
spills, whose twilit eyes brim
with the shadows of Sequoias—

is allowed to hear vespers
as if at a great distance
whispered from assembled stones

cold on a hill and dim
with candles: this
in the impulse of a dumb

maggot furious
at the base of his tongue.

Toward Night an Old Man Drove to Search

for rotted firewood. He'd started late
and from a hill above the darkened curve
where coastlands hunch along the sea, he made

uncertain guesses at where the house he lived in
stood. A closing lid of fog had changed
the ocean to a rumpled field of vivid

silent clouds. And as the coastland's shape
surrendered, on the hill he carried sticks
and crumbling, fungus-covered logs, laid

them in his trunk, then slammed it shut. At peace
he coasted down the road. The sun had faded
like an aging eye. He couldn't see,

with lights or without, and all the way
he breathed the wood's narcotic, ripe decay.

"In Late Winter"

In late winter, when stone-colored trees
steep longer in the tilting light—not yet green
as nuthard buds bundle-in unseen March red,
orange and yellow, bunches brightly locked
and swollen into nubs like toned Indian corn,
not ripe, but ripening—, I am drawn toward
water.

On the dock I walk while dust shakes
from sun-loosened boards. No one comes
while winter stuns the lake with rain.
Fallen specks, locked on water, float
indented into dimples such as needle-footed
insects prick in stepping the taut water's skin.
While the dust disappears, I bend and kneel,
looking through the face surfaces juggle.

While the Ocean Turns

I see
their long, thin stems

—straighter than the white ribs
of a perch
sea snails
have partially devoured
on a shelf-rock near the tide—

the thin, green
stems themselves
rising to my shoulder's height,
the fork of blooms widened
from the flower's green
narrow brain,

and know

the waves are taking
rotten flakes
like blossoms
from the perch's side

while Queen Anne's Lace
illuminates the hill, conceals
the sudden prospect of the cliff,
consumes me.

Light in a House of Mirrors
Considerations at La Push

Island high as our inland hills
John Logan

1.
I sleep in a clump of dark humped trees
where the river forks and roars below a bridge.

I sleep fitful as light in a house of mirrors,
dream of a drunken Indian
who sells me my own scalp slick as a skinned cat, dripping.

But when I wake and write to a friend
the dream I tell for her
is of a shape like my shape by the river,
filling slowly with a sunlight
bright as honey, quick as rain.
A tall attentive glow beside dark water.

2.
Here were the flatfaced people
whose earthfathers and earthmothers
circled toward
this land over a blue idea
of godliness
melting behind them, burning before.

3.
The flatfaced stones beneath my feet
predate Cezanne
longer than 10,000 redwoods end-to-end have lived
swallowing air and sunlight, rain and drifting
soil up into that gradual dance of the self
in whose shadow even longlived tortoise withers—

Split and fracture,
          dark falls of light
squaring edges of the once-round stone.
Scald and freeze of passion's glance and intellect's regard.

4.

A great ghoul grey from the ruin of a log
rose like mist before me
as I took my last steps back to camp, startling
as if to distract me from my story.
                    But no,
it was only my imagination, yellow-eyed and moss-faced
again.

5.

Once there was more land, higher than now. The
waters grew jealous, gathered their tribes and con-
spired. Men knew this and the strongest planned to
flee inland, leaving the others—the sickly and the
weak—to form a wall to hold back the waters. So
there they stood, the abandoned, and the waters were
indeed delayed before they rushed inland. Today we
can see the heads of the old ones at the shore here,
vast, moss-haired, silent. These were the runts, the
least of their race. And we feel dwarfed beside them.
For the strong ones, who were saved, shrivelled
among the safe places far inland. The heroes still
stand guard at the edges. We call them stones so we
will not remember. They no longer speak to us, who
are neither their sons nor daughters.

                              —La Push, Washington—

2. Inland

"that terrible vigilance"

Out There
for Charles Levendosky

Wind like a razor
slides over the smooth
cheeks of the plains.

In my car I feel conspicuous.

I stop to walk
and turn to watch
the road laid like a
frown of stone across
the endlessness of grass.
The idling car is fatally apparent.

No map I carry hints at this.

Later, driving on,
I wonder what it is
out there that notices
me as I pass,
what sensibility thrives
in all that terrible vigilance of grass.

In a Place So Empty
Hollow Bones Are the Only Hallelujahs

for Len Randolph

Here in the only Chinese restaurant for 150 miles
    all of us waiting for hamburgers listen
    to the latest on John Wayne's open heart.

The one flag in this town always unfurling is the wave
    of yellow dust aging billboards into WANTED posters.

Instahomes and trailers are flung across the spring prairies
    like a new deck of cheap cards that tatter at a touch
    and the whole town's one ongoing game.

Money cuts the deck.

Wind deals.

Each night stars range like headlights from
    a 3-D freeway in some lonesome cowboy's dream.

Bedrooms glow blue till dawn.

The newborn's heart can't beat, won't beat, holds its breath
    for a new start somewhere else.

We listen to Paul Harvey gust through static as the only
    pair of goldfish in Wyoming, both male,
    circle their bright coffin sinking slowly
    toward the live Chop Suey at the bottom,
    wobbling back up like feeble dragon-kites.

The hamburgers arrive. The fries are raw.

We all wear one expression.

The look of the traveler realizing
    suddenly he is on the wrong bus out of town
    and doesn't care.

                              —Gillette, Wyoming—

Nightshift

Cars parked outside lit plants,
patient as faithful wives,

waited to be unlocked, wakened
bright-eyed in the dark,

driven home.

Nightswim
for Rachel Goldstein

Perhaps it was because
with all their laughter
and the poolside lights
they disturbed a darkness
in the pruned sullen trees.

Two men, two women,
splashing in a dayblue pool
below stars hidden
in the glare they saw by.
Shooting like otters
down the slide, diving
like seals, each
wellfed and sleek,
regardless in their games.

When one man brushed absently
at a leaf that clung to him,
it bit: A tiny sodden
ghoul-faced bat. Like pins
the teeth and claws.
Tossed from the pool
to the pet cat, it
lay like a wet rag,

hissing among its wings.

For the rest of the night
that man kept glancing
at the dark, waiting
for another scrap of it
to seek him out.

In These Signs

Nowhere, late, the signs appear

SLOW

MEN WORKING

DETOUR AHEAD

and fresh scars on the earth
vanish as headlights
swerve, revealing
new mudflats in an old river.

END CONSTRUCTION
says the last sign, a yellow shining
innocent of itself.

Only coyotes
—bones arched round their hearts
like ribs of moonlight—
who live here night and day

are literate in these signs
they read by

bonelight, skullshine, bloodglow.

"Do You Know the Country Around Here?"

My people are like
deer
more than people.
My mother's aunt told me
this
just after I was born.
The first time.

She told me
she was 13 and—do you
know the country
around here?—her
mother
was at Sacramento,
called that now,
when the white man came there
a hundred years ago
or more
and chased them,
killing all the men
and raping
women they could catch.
The old and sick
and young.
The men died once,
the women
everytime. The women
lived.
      She was
13 then
and she hid under the leaves
and they came to Booneville,
they call it Booneville now,
and got away
and she didn't have to

hide in the leaves anymore then.

Our people are different.
My people are like the deer.
Nomads. They don't
settle like your people.
It was inevitable.
Your people are smarter.
Don't you think it was
inevitable?
I can see it in your eyes,
the way you are looking
at me now.

No, no, it's true.

Your eyes show me.

My people are like the deer.

—Healdsburg, California—

Teaching Among the Children of Chief Plenty Coups

Late October and in this country
the dry gold of the leaves
falls like old ornaments.
A Christmas that hasn't come
feels done with. Branches
reach into the air like roots,
and whatever blossoms
blossoms underground. Here
most faces are flat as the earth
and colors of the earth, and when their speech
erupts with Crow earth fills the air

as words the stomach somehow hears.

Speak, and you will be heard.
But question one of them
expecting what you would expect
of stone, or an old stump,
the wide blank gaze, neither
friendly nor hostile,
of a flat rock, or bark
with eyes. It is not
a gaze that isolates
a tree from its forest
or mistakes
words from the tongue
for the heart's talk.

What you want to know here
you must learn here
from that open book
whose quick words burn
on pages shed like leaves
in gusts of sunlight. And remember
that no leaf is the tree,
no tree the land; nor would
the land itself explain the curved
blue shield of the sky, the wheel
of the seasons turning, returning,
or the people who move freely still
among them all, alert
to the one wind moving
antelope and elk, eagle and owl
among their brothers
in the ritual of hunger, the hunters.

—Crow Reservation—

The Melon Vine and the Wild Berry Vine
for Gary Snyder

Established on the richest ground
the first is found in the valley
where the heavy wisdom of the rain
sinks gladly into darkened earth.
It labors to bring forth melons,
great melons sweet and crisp
for the daily feast of the harvest.

      If it is found the second is
      on hard slopes among thickets drinking
      thirstily at rain still silver
      before running off to the lowland.
      It labors to keep hold among stones
      as it brings forth tiny berries,
      bright yips of color in the wilderness.

Of the first notice how
its fruits are the easier gathered.
Looming huge on their vines,
accessible to the hired labor,
domestic, they gleam and shine.
Here one walks the easy fields
and tries the fruits and sits,
contented, in the sun.

      On high slopes harvest is difficult
      —the remoteness of berry from berry
      among dry thorns. Those
      who feed here soon grow lean,
      grow clever of hand and foot
      among treacherous rocks balancing
      delicately higher and higher
      above the fields, approaching clouds.

Below the wellfed sit melon-like
in the places of plenty
as shadows from the mountain

drift down late in the day
filling the dark with a darkness
the eyes of the fat shall not see,
charging the dark with laughter
the ears of the fat shall not hear—
though their daughters mingle there
making sons and daughters
the hearts of the fat shall not know.

Exploring Oneonta Gorge

Eyes bright as
backlit leaves,

here old gods
waded the gorge,

their deeply packed tracks
breaking into stones.

Balancing upon them
we walk on in

where no paths lead,
deeper and deeper,

each step
an unwitting prayer

to those we fail
to recognize gazing

back up at us
through the water's face.

Those before us,
those within,

those underfoot.

Reasons for Going it on Foot

I speed along knowing
the true journey

is on foot, hungry
and broke, learning

hour by hour local nuances
of accent and gesture

by which I may identify
myself as a stranger

eager to know
the ways of those

I beg my life from
as I pass.

X. ART & ARTISTS

"to consume appearance
at the speed of creation
as seen by stone"

"Innocence
has no part in the capture
of innocence"

Land's End

"The sun is God."
J.M.W. Turner's last words

1.
In this particular mindscape
god is light
god is light dissolving
stones sea and each horizon

The maps of recognition
are contrived of edges
and pretense

True tension shimmers

The skin of all being
delights in expanse

This last light opening
across the stone foundation
of Land's End excites response
as vital as the edge
of a lip across the
edge of a nipple

2.
This is not the end of land
seen by the habitual eye
accumulating detail
like a sleepwalker shopping
for a stuporous family

This is light gathering
to consume appearance
at the speed of creation
as seen by stone in its
gradual shudder toward sand

Not the definition
of what seems
but the radiance that haunts all immanence
the dynamic core glowing
the godheart

3.
For this is an act of worship this seeing through
this adamant gaze at the radical godlight
no church can admit
except through the mangle of frames and storied glass

And this is a going down to the knees
on rough Cornish stone no hand can soften
no ritual ordain
a prayerful apprehension among runes of opening
to light we may attend but never solve

as the lover dazzled beyond comprehension
accepts the beloved
among transformations consuming all
before history engages again

4.
Here god is light
whose worship is the eye altering all
the heart receiving and surrendering
bloodfire electric in a darkly pulsing place

This stone shines when light touches it
shines and kindles

until there are no edges on the earth

The Singing Tree
for Barry Lopez

In the forebrain of a Chinese male
in the year of the final voyage of Columbus to what he had
      first taken for India and then took for
tobacco, gold, and native samples to display
before the incredulous courts of Spain,
in that forebrain behind eyes
feeding upon an open field where a single horse
      stood beneath the single singing tree,
certain all but negligible disturbance took place
resulting in his application to a sheet of flattened rice
of a streak of compound consisting of ear-wax, the husks
      of various insects, spittle, and the juices of local herbs,
and as the stroke he laid down swerves
a horse lithe as a Siamese cat
rears, turns its elegant neck so that the head may neigh
frightening a longwinged bird from its graceful
perch of ear-wax and beetleshell, squawking
doubtless in perfect Mandarin dialect
      of the appropriate dynasty,
the whole work priceless now, its value at the current
      rate of exchange easily sufficient to
feed and clothe its maker for years who lived his entire life
poor as a rat, picking his ears for binder,
plundering his heart for the forms to stop time
in the figure of this rearing horse whose beauty
      all but stops my 20th Century Occidental breath.

Praise to the Sunlit Child Within

Dear Dylan, calf with the bull heart
    and wonder-spewing tongue,
how wise you were to waste no more
of heartbeat in flat labor,
    the conjugation of dead lung
and country weddings on the paper
acid and indifference so soon
    would bury in a beggar's cart.

In what pale chamber of the heart
    is blood filtered by fear
        and fashioned into wit?
        What simple dart
tossed by a boneless wrist
    so punctures brawling cheer,
        what distanced art?

To sing is the business of the blood
    foaming through slow bone,
to rant as rants the loud-eyed sun
without whose cosmic noise
    trees wither, oceans stale;
to give spirit its true expanse
and not annoy the guardians of genius
    with yet another drought that should be flood.

The child's eye is a brilliant star
    that brightens circling worlds
no stone-eyed fool can glimpse,
though stone may stare
    till Doomsday when the fiery glance
of some young god unfurls
    and Earth is ash in air.

Triangle

After a Painted Limestone Relief in the Tomb of Ti,
an Architectural Overseer; Saqqara, c. 2500 B.C.

Unrelievably vigilant, Ti
in limestone stands by Ti in dust.
The flesh on his bone (four thousand, five

hundred years entombed) is gauze on crust.
To hold his spirit, the Overseer's
pose is cut in stone. A papyrus

thicket behind his figure rears
bamboo-like stalks, corrugations
roofed by cluttered birds. Spears

are raised and a riverhorse flattens
its ears. Detached, a giant
Ti—poled on zigzag patterns

meaning water—observes the hunters
and a hippopotamus. The bottoms
of loaded boats skim the rumps

of huddling, scrambled beasts. Caught
in ropes, one squats improbably.
Twists its neck. Cocks its jaw.

Ti, eternal Overseer,
staff in hand, watches closely
the hunters' angled spears. Exactly

parallel, they juxtapose
against the boatman's pole, and static
shafts balance. *Control.*

Broken by a jaw, the basic
river-line provides the final
plane, creates the most fixed

and eternal form: an equilateral
triangle. Permanent
amid the agitated, vital

scene where fox-like creatures menace
nesting birds above the reeds
and riverhorses bawl at men

with spears, Ti, the Overseer
neither supervises nor
inspires the hunt. His figure seems

aware of every thing, divorced
from each. His body dead, its
spirit haunts a world scored

on stone walls. Time could stitch
his flesh with death, but Ti
had carved this tomb to mark his spirit.

Imperturbably alert, Ti
in limestone stands by Ti in dust
watching hunters, and watched by us.

Girl Near a Waterfall
after Suzuki Harunobu (1725?-1770 A.D.)

She is not thinking of being painted

This is why
my hands burn so, her spirit
trembling through this brush
my fingers become

Innocence
has no part in the capture
of innocence—what net

for birds
is made of air and song

She is the woman

I am the man

This is the canvas

"Jeunes Filles Au Bord De La Mer"'
after Pierre Puvis De Chavannes

Young women at the edge of the sea,
you say
in your title. That, and more.

You died an old man
in the year of my birth, you
who also lugged around
such a long name
all the days of your life.

Your women make me
touch my sunny flesh
with theirs. As one lifts
the brilliant whisper of her hair
from her fair shoulder,
another reclines
upon hers, its glossy mass
spread across gritty stone.
Those untouched breasts,
how they harden
my male nerve, soften my heart,
with their undefined nipples,
centers tender, warm and blind.

Can it be our lives are so contagious
one man may die, passing on

to another,
at birth, such a legacy as this
image of young women
brushing their hair by the sea, this oceanic
eye bluer than any
human could ever bear
looking through?

It is strange, is it not,
to be born to a name
not your own.

"In the North Wind of Le Pouldu"
Gauguin writing letters

1. 1889

I love Brittany!

Here I find
a wild
primitive quality. When
my wooden shoes
clatter
on the granite
I hear
that muted, dull and powerful
sound
I look for in painting.

2. 1889

I take my old body
for a stroll
in the north wind of Le Pouldu.

Of all my efforts this year

there remains only
the roar of Paris which discourages me
here to the point
I no longer
dare paint.
        The soul, however,
is absent and looks sadly
at the
gaping holes before its eyes.

Let critics take a careful look
at my latest work, if
they have the heart
for such things. They will see
what resigned suffering is.
                    Is
a human cry
nothing?

3. 1890

May the day come—and soon—
when I escape
to that island wilderness
        in the South Seas
where I can live
in art, ecstacy, and calm.

Far from the European money struggle,
surrounded by a new family,
there on Tahiti
        in those calm tropical nights
where I can hear my heart murmur
in amorous harmony

with the beings mysterious around me,
free at last,

with no concerns
        about money money money,
finally I shall be
able to love, sing, and die.

A Note on Nostalgia as the Corruption of Innocence
for ol' Fred

Problematic monsters tyrannize the mapped-out landscape
reeking with itself. The naked ark's aground,
grinding all to hell as the moon pulls
the hull of spirit, pulls
her over shoals of possibility, memory,
gradual corals encrusting her keel
until she's locked there, groaning,
her vital cargo starving in the dead lunar calm.

Idealist out in the Weather

When he opens his book, planes in his face shift
in its studied light. His voice
                    —tentative, abrupt—
unfurls like a flag declaring a new nation.
He crouches before us, a dark radiance
                    reading of friends, loss, ice,
and the land where hard men labor
coaxing new crops from exhausted earth
                    for a world devouring
wholly without regard for an idealist
out in the weathers of
                    spirit and the sky.
His sloped shoulders will not neatly fit
the one hollow suit he has kept
                    for weddings and funerals.

His is the unfashionable appearance
the rituals of attention and despair
                    impose on such a man
while the possees of high style, immaculately confidant,
declare the fashions in conscience,
                    the right modes for complaint.
And this one clearly is a veteran fugitive
who will not appear sober two days running,
                    whose slouch is powerfully insolent,
whose words are meant
to burn like hardwood in the winter of the heart,
                    whose awful hurt
is awareness of the open mouths of countless wounds
constantly charging indifference
                    as moths accuse the flame.
Gasping in the noose, still he will sing,
each breath a new start. Drunkenness
                    is the ax that mends his broken heart.

Waiting for Rain by the River
for Wendell Berry and Ed McClanahan

Wendell, back in Palo Alto again
where everything
from Leona the Spiritual Psychic
to El Camino Real
is named by signs and where faith
in signs is the fashion,
I feel like giving a name to the time
you and Ed and I sat
waiting for rain
by that river in Henry County.

I don't know the names of the road,
the river, the swimming hole
we sat by, the trees lining
the banks or what crop
grew in the fields behind us. And were
those tiny flowers blue or white,
or what? I just remember
once we'd sat there long enough
to quiet down and know the rain
would chase us off before much longer,
the world was quiet with us
and the only sound
was rain, soft rain starring
the river and the trees
reflecting there—until
that sound like a wet tent flapping overhead
and the sudden vision of the heron
flying upriver, toward us.

And that when he reached us
he turned and circled back
out of sight, calmly. It
changed us, not
so anyone else would know,
not even Tanya,
but so we knew. It was a moment

you live your life toward
that happens and is gone
before it has a name.
You said a minute later
it had been a sign. It was.
It was, and I have no name to give.

Next to the Fence
for Jack Cady

In the sideyard, which
he hadn't mowed since moving in,
he sat, reviewing fancies, as sunlight
shaped his body in its shining
skin. He smoked in quiet, tilted
back his head until the sky
was white and sheer, steep with light,
feeling all the wind that pressed him
through the bright hair on his legs
and arms and chest.
                        He nodded, nearly
slept, then a quail exploded
from its nest to the fence's corner post.
The eyes were dark, pearled with sight
and quivering as continental shapes
of black and white turned in orbit
in the socket of the skull. Its head was still.
It clucked and twittered, virtuoso,
while the cock-staff nodded on
its hood, a black note in the wind,
yielding to the fluid motion,
bobbing back to yield again,
back and forth, precise and atremble.
It clucked, waited, chuckled; cocked
its head, clucked again, and flew.
He closed his eyes to listen.
                        Charged
with seed, the tassles of dry grass

creaked among the leaves of weeds
like a wicker chair as someone
sleeps, half sleeps, and stirs. A pair
of grey wrens cleaned dried
bits of berries from their beaks,
tapped and scraped the resonant fence
to whet their bills like dull razors
on strop, then pecked the tall tan loaded
stalks of grass that rose along
the fence's open planks, drooping
and nodding, struck and shattered—broken
for their seed by sudden birds.

He rose to find his pen. The wrens
froze on the fence, flipped and vanished.
The sheen of light that shaped his body
in its own bright armor
disappeared. The wind relaxed;
and when he sat again, he found
his vision's artifacts were gone,
and he was deadlocked between silence
and the moment of shared song.

—Bolinas Mesa—

Snow

involves
irrelevance,
assumes forms *a priori*
    stone, tree,
    mountainside,

orders
the chaos
visible on slopes or
    fields and, falling,
    softens all

in light,
softens all
the hard dark necessary
    ledge of rock
    wound to the peak

and twigs
that branch down
through clenched earth,
    conceals and shines around
    the informed edge, the hazard.

Exorcism

In my fever I would dream, remember
nothing of the dream but darkness, heat.
And in my fear and darkness, I kept a candle
by my bed, and watched the shadows pulsing
till I slept and dreamed of darkness, heat.
Finally, on the last night, a fly woke
as I lay and tossed in the flickering dark.
I listened to it tick against the walls,
whir in the air, discovering limits
it neither remembered nor understood
as it ticked against the walls, whirred,
and I tossed, pulsing in my heat.
I slept, but woke to hear the candle
sputter with dry sudden wings. The flame
crouched, then leapt, widened at the base
and steadied while the room stank of singed air.
I woke in the morning cool, dreamless, diminished.

The Names of the Dead are Being Withheld Pending Notification

What if he's right, and these leaves of grass are thrust up
from the mouths of the dead
who kept their silence an hour too long?

Every one of us knows what could have been said.
Let's think about it, let's consider it now
while our mouths can still form their miracles

and at the edge of Earth's darkness
that constant green conspiracy gives off
mute sighs of oxygen to sustain our common tongue.

Choosing a Diamond

I.
The weather must
accomodate your purpose. A clear sky

is wrong. Strong light
disguises a poor cut, dazzles

the eye
without warrant. Ideally

the sky is overcast,
your own heart clear, the reservoirs

of light screened grey
through clouds level in the north.

2.
A fine history of local earth
—compressed by those dour ironists,

Heat and Weight—
is in the stone. It is

nothing but the ancient stuff
of swamps

long hidden from the sun, crushed
by subsequence

at a depth only
death survives in this conversion

of the stunned flesh
of fern and reptile

into these windows
revealing

their stored longing
for a light

more brilliant
than any living eye's.

3.
The ideal form
opposes

58 facets arranged
symmetrically to pass

light through a series
of planes

before it
blazes free. So prepared,

this stone is
the all-seeing Emersonian eye, its

perceptions innocent

of hungering intelligence.

It is all that remains
of forms

extinct now, evolved
into that eye

more perfectly dispassionate
than any saint's

and fit to meet
unblinking

the endlessly adaptive
gaze of God.

4.
Light, which speeds dauntlessly
through space to pierce

Earth's rind of air
and layered cloud,

passes slowly
through the diamond like old

memories through a mind
informed by new perspectives.

Wear it proudly then
on the brief gift

of your flesh,
knowing how

at the heart of such a stone
Time burns.

The Recognition
after Rilke

Lord, it is time. Our long summer ends.
Lengthen now Thy shadow on the sundial
and in the farthest fields revolve Thy winds.

Command Thy last fruits, that they swell and fill.
Give them two days more for their proud weight.
Urge them to fulfillment, then drive the sweet
chosen flesh into the rich wine of the fall.

Now who has no house shall build him none,
who is alone shall long remain alone
to wake and read, to write and read long letters.
Restless, he shall wander up and down
the shrouded avenues where leaves are swirling.

The White Hour of Pure Knowing

I do not know, none can,
What torturous illusions
In that unknown place
Occurred before the womb's
Secure red eye drew in
The soul housed by my face.

Bald monks, high in Tibet,
Who, cotton-clad and barefoot,
Can walk on stone through winds
That frost the yak's eyes shut,
Are said to know. And yet
Such answers, hidden in such minds

As theirs, exact as lasers,
Are remote as the Himalayas.
At first the upward path

Rises through banked hibiscus
Carved out of flesh by razors
It would seem, or drenched in the bath

Of blood drained from bones
Found further on. The ways
Once lit by flowering blur
Where heights airlessly blaze
And all the fragile knowns
Fail in the pure white hour

When wisdom burns to thaw
Icebright extremities
Back into bloom, when books
Flare in a heatless darkness
Countering the gaze of Awe,
Whose faceless Face looks

Out of stones or snow or the air
As Light peers from the fire
Or Snow stares out of snow.
As in a dream—not far
Now from the goal, nor near
Enough to touch it, so

To wake—, one gradually slows,
Cannot go on, or turn.
And void of all one knew,
With vacuum in the bone, one
Stares with eyes no longer eyes
From snow not quite yet snow.

The Dream

I dreamt that I would die
and could not wake. A space
of darkness, viscid, warm,
engulfed me—I floated. A fold

of fire split the dark,
gave vision, spilled
a shallow light that burned,
burned as I felt it flood

the swollen rim, and heard
a cry, then watched it issue
smoke and ash and fire.
It closed. I dreamt I woke.

XI. ON THE OTHER SIDE OF THE WORLD

"To create moon
in one's self"

Ouspensky

7 For a Magician

for Ray Rice

1.
Out of his black hat
he draws
rabbit after rabbit

and out
of the clear air
breath after breath.

2.
It takes him years
to learn
perfectly the poise
with which to reach
into his own sleeve,
withdrawing
the blaze of silk
it takes a generation
of mulberry leaves
and worms to spin
and the fingers
of strangers
to weave.

For the magician
about to astound
his audience.

For the lady
about to betray
her lover.

For the matador
into whose unborn wounds
first the horns
and scarlet scarf
then the faithful worm

must pass.

Applause.

He bows.

Applause.

*She cries out
to the dark.*

Applause.

*His eyes widen
as the horn sinks in
and in.*

3.
Who brushes
the magician's favorite hat?

The rabbit and the dove.

While he tends
to the hutch and scattered nest.

4.
His best makeup
is in our minds,
the hunger
of old locks,
rusted and lost,
to be opened.

Even skepticism
is a prayer
to him,
for whom fire obeys
the moon,

for whom water burns.

Imagine
the key of ice
designed to enter stone,
the lock made of mercury
which is its own pure key.

And look
into the clarified eyes
of just this one
who performs dreams,
who never sleeps.

5.
He brushes his teeth,
blows his nose,
eats with his mouth,
has but one suit of clothes.

He is very much like us,
it would seem,
to us.

6.
After each performance
he disappears.

Outside the stars brighten,
inside
the lights go on.

On the other side of the earth
it is morning
where he shares breakfast
with the chimpanzee,

who asks if it all went well.

They laugh as they eat.

7.
The last achievement
of an ultimate magician
is the proper
care and treatment
of all beings
filling the vast emptiness
of that hat
with which he lives.

—Mendocino—

Key to Poetic Forms

In the index of titles, an asterisk (*) will indicate each poem using a form other than free verse. Immediately after the title, in brackets, the form used will be abbreviated. The key to abbreviations is as follows:

[A]   / Accentual
[BV]   / Blank Verse
[C,r] / Couplet, rhymed
[FP]   / Found Poem
[I,4] / Iambic Tetrameter
[I,3] / Iambic Trimeter
[NF]   / Nonce Forms
[PP]   / Prose Poem
[Q,r] / Quatrain, rhymed
[R]   / Rondel
[S,r] / Sestets, rhymed
[Son] / Sonnet
[Syl] / Syllabic
[T]   / Tanka
[TR]   / Terza Rima
[T,r] / Triplets, rhymed
[V]   / Villanelle

Index of Titles

About the Author

William Pitt Root's seven collections of poetry include the forthcoming *Kingdom of Quick Song: Selected Odes of Pablo Neruda, Faultdancing* (1986), and *Reasons for Going It on Foot* (1981). Twice nominated for the Pulitzer Prize and the National Book Award, his poems have received three *Pushcart* Prizes as well as the Borestone Mountain, Guy Owen, and Stanley Kunitz Best Poem Awards. And his books have earned grants from the Guggenheim and Rockefeller Foundations and the National Endowment for the Arts. He's been a Stegner Fellow at Stanford and a United States/United Kingdom exchange artist for a year divided between London and Land's End.

His work has been translated into Russian, Hebrew and Yiddish (for broadcast over *Radio Free Europe)*, and into Japanese, Swedish, and Macedonian. In addition to translating Pablo Neruda, Root has co-translated *The Poems of Heinrich Boll*, and is at work on a book-length collection of translations and adaptations of miscellaneous poems from around the world, to be called *After Others*.

Root's work has appeared in hundreds of periodicals (including *New Yorker, Nation, Harpers, The Atlantic, APR, Commonweal)* and in over seventy anthologies. He's also published short stories, essays, and reviews. In the mid 1970's he collaborated with experimental film-maker Ray Rice to make two award-winning short films based on his poems.

Growing up first near the Everglades and then in the Pacific Northwest, Root has worked all over the United States: as a Teamster in Seattle and California, as a bouncer in the pre-World's Fair Pioneer Square, loading trucks in North Carolina, in factories, a shipyard, and an underground mine. Through Poet-in-the-Schools programs he has taught in Mississippi, Vermont, Oregon, Texas, Idaho, Wyoming, on the Crow, Wind River, Northern Cheyenne, Navajo, and Hopi Reservations. He has also served as Visiting Writer-in-Residence at Amherst College, Interlochen Arts Academy, the University of Montana, and as Distinguished Writer-in-Residence at Wichita State and Pacific Lutheran Universities. Currently he teaches in the Creative Writing Program at Hunter College in Manhattan, to which he commutes from Tucson where he lives with his wife poet Pamela Uschuk.

Cover art by Bruce McGrew
Book design and production by Tanya Gonzales
The type is Baskerville with Baskerville display
Printed by Cushing-Malloy
on acid-free paper